ABOUT THE AUTHOR

Linda Appleby is a native of Cambridge with Welsh roots. She was educated at The Perse School, Cambridge, where she was awarded both 6th Form prizes for English Literature and went on to gain a top Philosophy first of her year at Somerville College, Oxford. She taught English at South Worcestershire College and ran the college's language policy. Retiring on the diagnosis of a psychotic illness, she has devoted herself to her writing. She has written two novels and three poetry collections, as well as short stories and articles. Linda was married to Professor John Appleby. They have two sons.

Linda's book of poems, *Harvest*, was published by Austin Macauley in January 2022.

LINDA APPLEBY

the kingdom is yours

AUSTIN MACAULEY PUBLISHERS®

LONDON • CAMBRIDGE • NEW YORK • SHARJAH

A CIP catalogue record for this title is available from the British Library.

ISBN 9781035858422 (Paperback)
ISBN 9781035858439 (ePub e-book)

www.austinmacauley.com

First Published 2024
Austin Macauley Publishers Ltd
1 Canada Square
Canary Wharf
London
E14 5AA

FOREWORD

I've still got the diaries somewhere, scruffy from stuffing them in my handbag and covered with something just short of scribble. Five or six diaries. What was happening was earth-changing. I felt compelled to record it as faithfully as I could. Then, when my job was gone and I had £5,000 to support myself and the children, I wrote furiously at my son's computer in his bedroom, while the children watched videos – *Mr Bean*, *Home Alone*, *Apollo 13* – while munching crisps and Crunch Corners, or parked in front of the European Cup on TV until I joined them, all cosy on the bed-settee. The manuscript didn't even have to make conventional sense. As long as it was a true record. I knew it would make sense to those who were in the know. The analysts and theorists. Those who understood the runes of the unconscious.

I carried the print-out with me everywhere. I clasped it tightly in my arms when I was taken in an ambulance into hospital and kept it on the ward in a cardboard document box. If there was an influence on the writing, it could have been Anne Frank. Or now I see it as a kind of solemn Bridget Jones. Women in *extremis*, in a tragicomedy of manners. I had actually started writing the work in the classroom, sitting at the computer while the students wrote. That is where the 'story' starts. Then we look back to where the 'funny goings-on' began. I had taken a course in the theories of Melanie Klein at the Birmingham University Department of Postgraduate Psychiatry. I was mind-blown by the plethora of Kleinian meanings around me. Wrote a paper about the transition from paranoia to depression to sanity. And stepped onto a roller coaster ride of emotion and significance.

My degree was in Philosophy, Politics and Economics,

at Somerville College, Oxford. Mainly Moral and Political Philosophy. Then an MA at London, with a dissertation in Psychoanalytic Literary Criticism, which involved an assessment of psychoanalytic thought, as practised by Freud. And when the boys were tiny, I was shocked, gob-smacked, by the observation that the stages of development Freud described were being lived out in the developing child. Hence I enrolled for the course at Birmingham University.

My observations did not make me popular. Previous attachments withered. My husband left, and I had to soldier on. I went to a talk by the famous analyst Hanna Segal. She explained the theory of international relations. And pow! The world is changing! Why?!!! Perhaps the reader can, as I did, piece together an (or the) interpretation.

Linda Appleby, April 2024

The twenty-sixth of January 1988
A clear, blue, winter's day in Worcestershire – Thin strips of cloud form a mackerel sky.

I can only remember this murkily now but one day in that time of turmoil and tumbling inner feelings, a thought went through me that 'My unconscious is a television set.' This message, feeling, idea or item from the imagination made no serious impact on my intentions or beliefs. I had experienced so many ideas which I had allowed to pass and I would treat this one similarly. I did note this one, though. I believe I was lying in bed at the time.

The time I am referring to would probably be sometime in 1990 – I could check that, I think. It could have been 1991, after my paper was written on post-Freudian theory. It examined the connections between people, and their meaning. We are connected to our mother at birth. Are we all connected to a universal mother-figure? I suppose it would seem obvious that I did not connect the thought that my unconscious could be anything at all like this with the occasion that someone came from the Post Office and I was told that our house was emitting a colour television signal. I would have to pay the additional licence fee, because I had only paid for a black and white licence. The only television I had was a black and white set. Over the telephone to my ex-husband, Jonathan, we discussed the likely source of the signal. We were separated in 1988. An academic, he lives in Birmingham 20 miles away and sees the children at the weekend. He suggested it might be coming from perhaps the next-door neighbour's house. I must say I wasn't convinced.

That is how things began, but it wasn't until one of my visits to Mr Lowery that I remembered that 'unconscious TV' thought and managed to speak it and consequently put it away. Ian Lowery was a Freudian psychoanalyst who was helping me on matters of the children's care following the split. His face told me it was not a thought to be given a public airing. Later, though, I did, when other occurrences showed me that I might associate this impression with similar events in the world, and I began to wonder what the connection might be.

Summer 1990

This is not a fiction which I have come to record. It couldn't be. I have not, for a long time, been too interested in stories. Still less, in inventing them. A personal penchant for the theoretical, I mean.

My life's instinct, drive, unstoppable epistemophilic urge was toward the logical conclusion, the well-fitting, verifiable argument. I shot out of my mother, with a short, four- or five-hour first stage and an uncontrollable delivery, she said. Collected a lot of barnacles around that urge in the first few years, which I have spent the last few years sloughing off. And that is the starting point for this tale.

Joe is our elder son. He is 7 when the story begins. A very happy, generous child who helps me since his father is absent. He finds matters of religion and the supernatural to be ridiculous. Henry is our younger son, aged 3, a placid child who attends Mass daily with his Catholic childminder. I am a Lecturer at an Adult Education College.

I know that some taxis had something to do with it. My life had dropped into a slurrious pit, quite suddenly and for no reason. One day I was painfully doing so well, getting the children ready in the morning, Shreddies, socks, dinner money, psychoanalysis of son merely to remain emotionally stationary, just being a mother, averagely put-upon, alone, loving, hating, pleading, pushing, hoping mother, and the next day the bottom had dropped out of my world. Along with the petrol out of my car. – I ended up taking a taxi to get some more. My life had stopped.

I just can't get the Second Coming out of my mind. Since I took up Kleinian/Freudian activity every meaning has had its two meanings; simultaneously; separately and together. Coming; coming; and the sum or multiple of coming and coming. The smashed metaphor. The expanded metaphor. Try talking to someone like that.

There is quite a straightforward story, one of meeting a woman whose name brings cheer to my heart, Dr Hanna Segal. There is a beautiful myth I have been told which I am daring to place alongside it, shuddering with the hunch that the two might be connected. Dr Segal is a psychoanalyst in the forefront of the analysis of schizophrenics. She is a follower of the analyst Melanie Klein.

The end of the world, or Armageddon, or Judgement Day, or Peace on Earth and Goodwill to All Men. I can't actually find a Christian who has a clear line on it, except the people who deliver *Watchtower*. But my childminder told my she had heard of a prophecy concerning three women, one of whom is very old, unfortunately. She would pass the secret on, via the woman intermediate in age, to the youngest, I think.

Christ is among you. Ye will not know him. One of the reasons why you will not know him is because I think He may be a Her. Christ was a Jew. Poor and oppressed, most say, he was the son of a carpenter. Christ is among you and He is a mother. O ye of little faith. She is singing the songs and kissing the wounds of her loving, needing, fighting kin. She is living every minute of, acting out, almost literally, Christ's sacrifice. She will be brought before a trial. And God will find words to put into her mouth. You need not be afraid.

(There will be no revolution without women's liberation, we used to say.)

I was tempted by the serpent and I did eat. But what would we have learned if I hadn't? There would have been precious little to exercise the epistemophilic instinct. I learned about good and evil and shame. But also the good beyond evil and the innocence beyond experience.

My sister Rosemary told me that Hanna Segal would be speaking locally at the CND national conference. I was delighted. Dr Segal wrote the introductions to my books on Melanie Klein. The books I had ravaged and savoured through 1990. She was one of the first to attempt to analysis of schizophrenics. My teacher's teacher. I attended the session: 'The Need for an Enemy'. I figured out that Hanna Segal would be talking about the paranoid defence against a psychic split. After all, what did the Conservative Party do after the Cold War had ended? When mega-Germany could no longer be peddled, as a threat? And nobody cared about the ECU? What happened when barren months in the desert did not bear the fruit of war with Iraq and the hostages were coming home?

The party split. It didn't just split any old way. As Klein could have predicted and I was just beginning to understand, it split right down the middle. Those greedy, permanently warring, wounding internal parent-figures inflicted such a hurt on the party that it needed a Nice Man to heal those wounds. What it got was John Major. Everywhere I looked, I could see 'Nice Men' healing real or imagined splits.

Hanna Segal was little, old and very wise. The other members of the panel were buzzing with that justification of aggression which Dr Segal was about to explain. Which they would not understand. Dr Segal was introduced as the 'doyenne' of British psychoanalysis. I was so proud. Such a dignified affirmation that in all my explorations I had not disappeared anywhere at all. She explained the Kleinian mythology: the furious baby projected, split off from the idealised breast and held apart for the sake of internal balance, maintained by the ideal, until the whole Mother and reality. She had a mid-European accent. She talked with ease about Ze Loony Bin, and I at last was not afraid.

A God of love, nature and justice.

Then the secret: that group relations functioned on this paranoid level. That international relations followed this crazy course. We went camping at the seaside. Communist

11

Russia collapsed. I thought back to the protests in China, and the fall of the Berlin Wall. Things were changing in an impossible way. This impinging reality. How could it be happening on such a scale?

Later 1990

On the way to Mr Lowery in Birmingham; Sunday, at Corley Service Station on the M6.

My mind is containing Jonathan's and it is in four parts. I told Mr Lowery. He said, 'Don't you think you ought to tell him, so that he knows what's going on?' I didn't tell him. I thought he would shoot me to pieces. Three months later, Jonathan was recovering from a suicide attempt in Selly Oak Hospital. The day we would have been in court. 'I don't know why I did it,' he said.

Things which were happening inside were beginning to happen outside, too.

Also, in the summer of 1990

I went to visit Rosemary and Philip, just for some company and perhaps because I was feeling so scared. I sat on the green sofa and talked to Rosemary. She had taken no interest in the Freudian thing, had done rather well to tell me about the conference, but there I was, telling her that 'something is taking the paranoia out of the world' as if she would understand. She put her hands together in a gesture which seemed to be of prayer, but was probably one of despair and terror and said, ' I love you, L.,' meaning, perhaps, 'You are quite mad and lost and I want my old sister back.' Philip and some colleagues rushed wildly around. My life descended, into the slurrious pit.

Social Services – a Court Welfare Officer – Solicitors – Mr Lowery – the Personnel Manager – letter upon letter upon letter.

And then in Ian Lowery's room, cool, blue, with a carpet of squares, a blue couch, a square of carpet contained a blue heart. My eyes landed on it. That is it. They will not stop until they reach my heart. And I don't know what I said, and I had vaguely, privately noticed this before, that out of the corner of my eye, in association with my inner feelings, stirring inside me, I noticed that the sun shone.

Encouragingly.

Mr Lowery bowed his head, and moved his chair obliquely, in a movement perhaps of reverence.

Diaries – internal and external events, clanging and singing in time with the cosmos – a changing world. Students arrived from across the globe, war refugees, unaccustomed travellers, bringing stories of upheavals from Yugoslavia to Korea.

I sat in the upstairs room at the multi-cultural education centre and welcomed each new member of a kind of upstairs war cabinet or committee of discipleship forming a bridge across Europe and Asia, over to Osaka and crossing the Pacific Ocean to the Southern Andes.

'Hallo, I am from Ethiopia. I am a Christian.'

'Hallo. I am from Argentina. My friend is a nun. She meditates and goes to market and buys an avocado every day.'

I thought that Alan would marry me. He is a History lecturer in the Academic Education Department of the College, where I teach. His wife, Rosanna, teaches French. I thought that his wife was a poor second to me and only such factors as money and children would stand between us. My brother was leaving his wife for a greater love and I felt that this was – though a difficult thing – an honourable one. Our own father had made a similar move though later in life and we had learned to understand to forgive and to live with. I had not met people who thought that my apparently humble aim would qualify me to be dismembered and cooked in an oven and to whom life was a static misery dedicated to the social display of doing the right thing. I had freed my own husband – in fact, it looked as if I had fallen in love with someone from a litigious group of axe-grinders and I quite quickly fell out of love with him. He dumped me and he went on to kiss me passionately at my desk. I took him to the pub to ask him, quietly, not to do that again. He kissed me, laughing, in the car park. The following day, he kissed me passionately while I was reading my post in the office. Any lie was sufficient to hold up the edifice of his family and career and destroy mine.

I hit him, gently, for his lies… he being a foot taller than me. He pretended to be offended – this had, in fact, given him the story he needed for his wife. They gave 'evidence' that I was attacking them and I was given a final written warning. Divorced women– a place where unwanted emotions are dropped with no shame. To the public eye his wife was as wronged as Hero and I was unwillingly Bianca.

My ex-husband took up the theme.

The war between Serbia and Croatia was threatening to head for Bosnia-Herzegovina. My Croatian student, Mark, repeatedly drew me maps, Montenegro, Slovenia… when it gets to here, it will be appalling – there are three sides, all fighting against each other. Mark's parents were divorced, one being Croatian, the other Serb. He had been a soldier in the Croatian army, returning to Britain where he had lived as a child. Mark had told me about the Serb soldiers. 'They're crazy. They're just roaming round the countryside, drunk, raping women.'

My Asian friends. As those around me were trying to rock my boat and blow my house down there were my trusted envoys from the Hindu religion, the Sikh religion

and the Muslim religion who were each, as I juggled
their fascinating ways and requirements, unendingly
enthusiastically teaching me what I would need in
endurance and poker-faced acceptance. At the end of this,
Coventry Cathedral was perfectly placed to take up the pain
and the conflict, the church as described by Philip Larkin,
ironically in his atheism, as

> 'A serious place on serious earth…
> In whose blent air all our compulsions meet.'

I looked at the face of Christ moulded from the metal
of a crashed car. I stood at the screen of the Chapel of
Gethsemane. I walked along the avenue of stone tablets
carved with messages from the past, being now predictions
of the future and living statements; I am the comforter,
come alive.

> Pree-ee-ee-pare ye the way of the Lord
> Pree-ee-ee-pare ye the way of the Lord

I shuddered at the wording of the letters embedded in the
floor: 'I am among you, as one…that serves.'
   There was oil for healing. I looked at the tapestry, as
everyone does. 'Terrible,' had said our Swiss friend twenty-
five years earlier – I thought she had thought it was dreadful
– and I had learned to take an interest in it. I noticed that
in the four corners of the rectangle on which Christ so
roundly, femininely sat were four symbols, the signs of the
gospelmakers. I could fight the application Jonathan had
made for custody of our three-year-old and seven-year-
old sons. I had spoken to Mrs D. in London. I can only
remember her name as Mrs Dresden, though I know it is
not her name, she being, I suppose, small, delicate, pretty

and much maligned and she had warned me, 'Once they're out of the house, that's it.'

'Whose sons will rule with a rod of iron.'

Life is Karma. It is like a car. It has four wheels. We live on the wheel of our destiny. We live our Karma. We do not even tell of it.

(Christmas Humphreys, Buddhism, and Bhanumati Patel, GCSE coursework. She is the secretary at the Multi-Cultural Education Centre.)

'Look! this is all about Hindu religion!' Hemlata Patel, teacher of Gujarati and student of mine in English. 'Here is a picture of Gandhiji.'

Everything just is.

We are all equal. There is no caste or gender difference. There were ten gurus. The tenth one was forced to set up an army, to defend ourselves.

(Gurdeep Garcha – GCSE-assessed talk. She is the Bilingual Liaison worker at the Multi-Cultural Centre of the College. I have taught her GCSE English. She is a respected Sikh who reads in the Gurdwara or temple).

Respect, respect, respect. Prayer and respect, and fasting and pilgrimage. The pillars of Islam. Respect for women, for education with safety, respect for a woman's body.

(Abbas Khalifa – He is learning English for Islamic purposes. He is a Molvi at the mosque, a sumptuous purpose-built building in Nuneaton where the local Gujarati Muslims worship. He is teaching me many aspects of Islamic and Gujarati culture.)

We live in a happy state of chaos.
(Auntie Beryl 1996)

'God si love.' The ghee is sliding down the Sikh man's nose. Dear E M Forster would have enjoyed all this, I think. These are the same people we read about in *A Passage to India* at school.

We will do something which will suit everyone.

There were connections, in any case, and method or purpose in it all.

There had been the Gulf War, too, when Alan and I had fallen in love with each other the year before and now a series of men emerging like moles from underground: Brian Keenan, Terry Waite and John McCarthy. I had not enjoyed the criticisms of Terry Waite, which had accused him of naivety in making a peace mission to Beirut and felt it was far from inevitable that he too would be kidnapped. There was every reason to make a simple and humane plea in the most direct fashion, in the spirit of conciliation, this being the point of the message. I have never forgotten his account of his receiving a postcard depicting John Bunyan in prison, which was sent by a woman in Bedford. I wonder, was that woman Ruth?

In August 1990, I met Peter.

The name came back to me later.

Peter Poplar. A journalist on the *Independent*, who I met on holiday in Lancashire. He is to become the paper's correspondent in India, writing particularly about the war in Afghanistan. Latterly, he has been their correspondent in Rome. I don't know why he had such a powerful effect on me.

I met him at the Summer School at Lancaster University. He told me he wrote for the *Independent* – which I had never read. There had been some references to the Pendle witches and I was metaphorically being tried for witchcraft. Peter had spent the previous evening at Lancaster Prison for some reason. Perhaps a tour. He was wearing a blue and white striped shirt. I met him on Thursday 9th August.

The following morning a journalist who famously wore a blue and white striped shirt and who had spent five years incarcerated in Beirut was free, it appeared in the newspapers, the journalist being John McCarthy.

Peter and I had talked about our divorces. We were both concerned about possible problems with the children. I reassured him about the efficacy of psychotherapy.

Somehow I had missed Nelson Mandela. I remember Hamida Khalifa telling me about it; she was a member of the local Muslim community, Asian girls' youth worker and student of English. She had spent a Saturday morning watching television, waiting for Mandela to be free, telling her children about the importance of this event in history. It was Hamida, too, who told me that an aubergine had been found in a Leicester greengrocer's which, when split open, read 'Allah' in Arabic. But I do remember Mrs Truckle, the lecturer on the psychoanalysis course I took at Birmingham University, child psychotherapist, telling me of Mandela's release that he must have an enormous amount of 'good object'; most people leaving prison after so long would only be able to tolerate a clear, white room. And when I left our home for a smaller one, so that Jonathan could buy a house of his own with his share of the profits, I placed a poster in one of the upstairs windows which read 'The Struggle Is My Life.' Even so, it was several years before I understood our neighbours' deep prejudice about our way of life, which had destroyed the trust in our marriage.

And I wrote at the time, on the twelfth of August, the glorious twelfth 1991, that: these things are now familiar to me, but not readily transferred into words, even written. It is all too astonishing, and should be unbelievable, but the patterns and frequencies of 'coincidences' are too convincing to ignore. I have not wanted to believe it – but when I do believe it brings me great peace.

That weekend, if I go to The Bible, is of significance. On Friday, Peter. Did not have faith, know me. He betrayed me in the night (but I've done this twice before, he said). We had fallen out. He did not want to see me again. Was it the collision over the Japanese and the Welsh?

Perhaps he wept, bitterly. Perhaps he knew me in the morning. He said, 'There's something inward-looking about you.' But I was annoyed with him and ignored him. I see him standing there apparently wanting contact and me blanking him out. I can't remember why, now, what the row was about. That feeling. And his mother. An elderly woman hopeful (she had left a place for her son, next to me, at dinner) and on the rakish side. A blonde forty-year-old man. A boy of Japanese appearance, the three sitting down in the morning to eat breakfast.

Came home. Depressed. Elated. Force depression into anger; maybe it will save me. Yesterday I told Ian about some of it. I can't remember where I brought in 'Do not touch me.' It just came to me. I had wanted to say 'Noli me tangere.' I looked it up last night. Last night I found the passage in Matthew which said 'Christ calleth Peter.' I couldn't find Peter.

– It's all pastiche, for goodness sake. The plan is completely arbitrary, it's just whatever happens, to me, and nothing to do with any proper purpose.

I must look up all references to Peter. It is the exercise of accident, and free will working its way through the universe. It is RUTHLESS. Christian existentialism. I am without Ruth. She was a lecturer in English with me, a tower of strength as a colleague, recently leaving college because she was not happy there.

This morning; resurrection on the third day. Mary and Mary. Peter's denial. He goes to see where Christ's body is lying. The body has gone. Peter came back for his jacket. I had found his surname in his wallet – and lots of dollars. I was on the way to the loo at the time. When I returned he, too, had gone. He is the rock on which the Church is built. So/ just symbolic/ so who is Dan?/ Who was Daniel? A prophet who seems to be concerned with rivers. I met him at camp. At Lancaster, we studied Tippett.

Who he actually was was my partner after Jonathan left, a microbiologist, son of the humourist Ivor Cutler, with a cuttingly critical take on politics and high standards for himself and others. I still feel the force of his conscience.

> Deep river
> Deep river
> I want to cross over into
> Camp ground.

I began to clean Peter's spirit. He is the rock, the first I could reach, perhaps.

Do not touch me.

> Touch me not, for I am not yet ascended to my Father
> Matthew 20; 17

> Do not touch me: I am not yet risen to my Father's house.

I think I see. Well, Peter wrote his father's obituary about eighteen months ago. Peter as Posthumus, *Cymbeline*. It fits the narrative. No wonder they are afraid.

One thing I could do with Peter was to follow his writing in the newspaper, starting with a piece on the development of the London docks, 'a development opportunity two-thirds missed,' reminiscent of Joseph Conrad's opening to *The Heart of Darkness*, which describes the Thames, reaching from its English estuary to the heart of the Belgian Congo, and Marlow's adventuring. His discovery of Mr Kurtz' logical and heartless kingdom... The article referred to the connection between things. I was sure he was writing from his meeting with me. I turned to the Sunday supplements.

Could I really have had that sort of marriage? I thought of Islington's Georgian squares and sang one of my favourite songs to myself. Public schoolboys wearing white scarves, parties and taxis. This had also been my world, alongside the student... accommodation and demonstrations, or camp, or at home in Cambridge. I reclaimed it a little, even from here. I wrote to Peter at the newspaper, received a puzzling reply; nothing more. He was away on his own voyage of discovery and I admired his courage. For seven years his spirit has come back to me. We had danced together to 'Out, demons, out'. Once he wrote that he was re-converting to Christianity – I thought of him as a figure like C S Lewis and dreamed that we would meet for tea at The Randolph, the hotel in Oxford.

In 1991 I stood in the huge, sandy cavern of Coventry Cathedral, smelling the walls' perfume, and begged 'Show me the way'. The answer came resonating back to me; it said, 'I am the Way, the Truth and the Life.'

Material from 1991

Saturday 22nd September

Warwick University bar.

I don't like it here very much, but it is useful to be able to listen to people. They give me clues as to where it has all got to.

I am thinking generally of Jonathan and sibling rivalry. How a couple can be in competition; Serbia and Bosnia as sibling rivals, struggling for independence and recognition, self-realisation.

'Tomorrow is Pentecost, when the Holy Spirit enters the disciples.'

On the way home from here ('My wife won't let me' – Alan) it started raining!

Monday 23rd September

The problem was that my family tried to steal my elder son, Joe. They could not admit that they had undermined our relationship. They could not see that you don't just throw family relationships away; you work on them.

Thursday 26th September

It is my sister Rosemary's birthday. She is thirty-nine today.

She sees me as Saddam Hussein, the Devil. And herself as Israel.

And Henry, our younger son?

Monday 30th September

'Do not be motivated to avoid failure. Turn it over...be motivated to succeed.' My students start to sneeze.

Saturday 5th October

Last night a decision to separate Serbia and Croatia.

Today, a breakthrough in peace is announced. The countries will revert to their original boundaries.

I went to a performance of Haydn's *Creation* in Coventry Cathedral.

The Provost, John Petty, told us how Christ made people whole who met him.

He whole-object related.

I am more able to face pain. It is ebbing away.

I love the messages on the tablets in the new cathedral. One about the shepherd, one about the vine.

The lighting was beautiful, at one end, the tapestry and at the other, the windows, darkness, light. Emrys was in the choir. The English lecturer at Birmingham University. I felt that he had seen me. I felt warm in the light.

Sunday

I read Betty Joseph's *On Understanding and Not Understanding*. I feel more stable, multi-layered...

Monday 7th

A video of the hostage Terry Anderson was released. I had written to Peter yesterday. Peter – prisons – men in jail. Prisons or marriage, of the mind, or neurosis.

Tuesday

I saw Alan's wife, gloating, but something clicked. The sky cleared. Serbia, Croatia and Slovenia are independent.

There's the college fire bell again; I take it to be signal anxiety (Alan's). The fear is that the castrating mother will kill Alan. The sun is coming out as I write. The sun is coming out through the mist. Is Margaret Thatcher dead? Later, at home, I found that Margaret Thatcher had been prevented from speaking at a conference.

At about five o'clock Josephine, the childminder, tells me that 'I had a dream about you.'

The message is 'Just knock on the door and he will be there for you.'

Thursday 3.30

The sun is coming out. The birds are singing. We can all be free.

Saturday 26th October

Jonathan came to see us. He was sorry for what he had put us through. He felt he had lost his future. I said little, but was happy to have some contact. He seemed surprised that I had now become distant from him. That that person no longer exists.

Jonathan's mother rang and did not talk much. I felt Peter wishing that Karyn Smith, the alleged drug-smuggler, could be let out of prison in Singapore. A more reliable ceasefire was announced in Dubrovnik.

My birthday

Joe told me his dream. Alan came out of the newsagents with a comic and it was called the *Beano* and he crossed the road but he wasn't looking and the bike crashed. He was badly hurt and the doctor came and the boy who was reading the comic took no notice.

Alan gave me too much power and then fought that powerful person.

November 11th Armistice Day

The message is:

Love your father.

So it goes on, thinking interpreting, recording, making links between messages and theories, internal impressions, external events, sometimes rather hoping that I do not get this wrong. I can see the resistance when I close my eyes and I can hear the words or thoughts and unwrap them. In some way, this must all pre-planned. I try to fathom that out.

Well, by the end of 1991 I had fought off this round of legal challenges, but I was not under any illusions about the origin of my 'good fortune.' I must lift up mine eyes to the hills, where my help comes from.

An aeroplane crashed in Sweden today. Everyone survived. They said it was a miracle.

They saw the hand of God. But few will know that it was a miracle indeed, and not merely a happy event. It has taken two thousand years to fulfil those wants. To make possible the things we wanted instantly. God has waited for two thousand years. I can wait too.

I feel like travelling again.

The 'News At Ten' on Radio Four: I see Bridget Kendall as the link between myself and Peter. She was the Moscow correspondent through that summer, as the Soviet regime disintegrated and when Boris Yeltsin climbed onto a lorry in Leningrad, perhaps with as much of the purpose as he has shown since, but with quite some courage. Peter and I had mentioned Bridget – someone I had known of at school.

I am overwhelmed when I hear the word 'connected.' I feel an awful guilt and responsibility, as well as excitement. Let me explain: my paper was about umbilical connection; a relation prior to that of the breast. The baby fantasises feeding the mother through the umbilical cord; a feeling of self-importance from the loss of which we struggle to recover. But which can be replaced by a feeling of connectedness. We are all being connected, are establishing a worldwide virtuous circle.

On December 29th I went to see *Dances With Wolves*, a film about being on the frontier, learning from the native, cross-cultural communication. A frontiersman befriends an American Indian group, marries one of them.

John Cole is saying on BBC1 that Saddam Hussein is still there and we are hearing about the Kurds. Who is the real Whore of Babylon? The wife or her usurper? My mother is reading at the Quakers: I said to the man who stood at the gate… We have talked about the 'light' of Quakerism. They say 'find a light' in people. It is like the light of enlightenment in psychoanalytic theory. The light of the world.

7.43: Joe said 'connect' for the first time. He said that his exploding egg would connect.

From envy to a sublimation: connect?

'Go out into the world in peace.' 'Render unto no man evil for evil.'

Other material from 1991

Really there was a lot about siblings and the fighting greedy parents, struggling towards sweetness, perhaps, and sweet smells and incense. I taught more Croatians, illegal immigrants perhaps, doctors who had escaped soldiers through toilet-windows, couples wanting to perpetuate that emergent Mediterranean lifestyle abroad, then Rumanians, Bosnians, the unforgettable Vera and Vjeko from the Sarajevo School of Music and a Russian and, in a different class, a Serb. A different sort of chaos with the Bosnians; not a happy acceptance, just disorder, though not through any fault of their own.

The Year of Our Lord 1992

On the first of January John Major, the Prime Minister of Britain, expressed the opinion that it is now inconceivable that there could be a war in the West.

So what did people think had happened? Did we remember this tide of feeling towards peace when another Gulf War was threatened eight years later? Or was that not a war in the West?

'We are no longer living under the nuclear overhang which has affected this generation so much.'

The explanation for these things 'goes down' very badly just at the moment.

But Dr Fish, a Coventry psychiatrist, says, 'Don't you see a new revulsion against war?'

I dreamed that Adrian Millington's painting was all right, but the bottom of the picture was not in perspective, unlike mine. Woke. Jonathan had said that the overdose 'had put things in a new perspective'. His paintings have always been two-dimensional.

The connection is an electrical connection.

I love the thought of a God of Nature and not just of peoplekind; derived from, out of Nature; God as creator of the natural world and not just of His people; the idea of God of the Hindu religion, and early Welsh pantheism. That the Christian god is a Hindu God and Jesus is an avatar; a form of Lord Krishna, a few years before nought, Palestine. A view which shows women as creators and providers of comfort, men as fertility figures. We have a strong feeling of Jesus within and in control of nature. The waves parted, the winds calmed. We have a stronger feeling for Jesus' connection with Nature than for that of any other religious figure in history, perhaps. The only other who comes to mind would be one of His followers, Saint Francis of Assisi. However, a Franciscan friar told Rosemary and myself that this reputation was not well-founded and that he should be remembered more for his work with people than with animals.

'Where is God in your world picture, Rosanna? I suppose that He is conflated with you. Your view of God is that of a toddler; You are God to you and He exists to do your will.'

But He has a purpose for us all. He has a purpose for me, too, and I seek only his will. Jesus gave us a new commandment, and this was one of compulsory love. Without love and its forgiving instincts we are as a sounding bell.

Jesus said to the woman from Bethany, 'Go and sin no more.' And I am not the woman at Bethany. I am not without love. Not love willy-nilly, but perhaps if something is really special...?

And where is The Truth? Another Rosa, Rosalind, Shakespeare, took on another identity; a disguise, did she not?

A passage in Corinthians tells us that we may divorce the unbeliever. And I did not divorce Jonathan; but we may divorce the unbeliever because God's love is greater than these things, and all we need is to have faith in His Will. Two slightly bald patches underneath my hair remind me of this.

They stop exactly where they cease to become visible. And the gaps in my teeth disappear, just where my smile begins!

The wages of sin is death. The wages of falsehood is ten times of this.

Repent and ye shall be saved.

Peter's impediments had been: 'You are too clever for me.' This was a variation on an opinion of my colleagues that I am too stupid for them. He was worried because 'You mentioned Oxford' – as one is wont to do – 'and other things.' Not that I was obsessed with finding a husband!

It's just…that one puts one's mind to these things.

What I hear in my mind's ear is: 'I tried to pick up a psychiatrist!' Well, I can think of little other comfort or professional response than to explain that, well, these things happen.

Then there was the question of race. He laughed at me, saying I was Welsh, I felt a little uncomfortable about the Japanese; I hadn't met Tetsoya yet. Just a slight misfiring between us.

These were the years of arranging and re-arranging, in carrying household objects from one room to another.

Each action was acquiring a ritual meaning. I knew that God was in every movement, in actions of the most commonplace purpose. God was with the ordinary woman, simply in carrying laundry and moving plates. I embraced this as my lot. It was not safe to employ a cleaner any more, it seemed. People who came into our home had a habit of metamorphosing into spies, gossips, enemies. From the Hindus, I was given the idea of 'karma'. This, and in no other way, is how things are. They just 'is'. Seek what is of God; seek what is meant and pursue it. What does God want to show me in this? He wants me to look after everything. It is given for you. He is telling me to care for the animals, the cats and the birds. Feed them with all of your mind. From the Sikhs, I received the idea of The True. What was there before the Big Bang? What was there before the burst of creativity which started off what we know? Before the Big Bang was The True, which was and is the Word.

'The gifts of God for the people of God.' Said John Petty, the Provost of Coventry Cathedral.

I learned how to honour the moment. That is to pause and to honour things as they are, at this moment, to the glory of God. Mark it. I learned to stop and to see.

'Behold, I am making all things new.' I wrote to Ruth: 'The world is, indeed, being made new.'

As I carried household objects from one room to another, one part of the cosmic psyche to another, Creation re-arranged itself. Creation re-asserted herself. The broken was being mended and the partial now made whole. I have an article by Peter, dated 18th July 1992. It appeared in the Saturday magazine. It was on the subject of the prisoners of Dartmoor (Peter's theme, prisons; and keys), who were given the task of breaking rocks. The rocks; were they the impediment of *The Franklin's Tale* – an invented impediment, elaborate refusal or excuse? I would marry you if…when all the seas run dry…you could move these rocks.

In *The Franklin's Tale*, Aurelius does indeed move the rocks. He employs a magician. Dorigen learns to regret her flippant promise. Or do the rocks represent a real impediment, as with Mr Rochester, 'I am already married'? Well, Peter is the rock. Marriages falter – they are 'on the rocks'. Romantic heroines, according to Chaucer, shout rhetorically at them and throw themselves at them. Do they represent the inevitable? Well, what Peter wrote was that Dartmoor, with its 'fearsomely powerful architecture', its defences, 'refuses to go away'. I was enjoying his writing, thinking about his references and associations. It was in 'the public arena'. Unfinished business is unfinished business, for everyone.

Then towards the end of the year, the theme of the service for Armistice Day at the cathedral was reconciliation; reconciliation within the Church on the subject of the ordination of women. You can imagine my sense of dislocation. Something about the bombing of the old cathedral and reconciliation with the mother. The need for change and movement: to move my troops onto another plane and not be shouting at God any more. I could taste wine. This is all so attenuated and not a struggle any more. Not the 'working-class struggle' – we begin to wonder what that was and why this simple girl should have any part in it.

It becomes a process; not a dialectic. I do not drink wine.

15th Nov.

I am disappointed. We could have gone out with Billy this weekend, or to St George's Hall, in Nuneaton, for Ivan's family wedding party. Ivan is a new part-time lecturer at the college, converted to Catholicism after being cured of a disability as a child. Billy is someone at work now; quite charming and attractive, though perhaps not a teacher. Not at all a teacher, it seems, as by the end of the term he has left and we find that he has misrepresented his qualifications.

This weekend is another one of those times when nothing is said. There is imagined to be an 'understanding'. But there isn't. And somehow the 'understanding' is simultaneously negated, too, to save embarrassment, I suppose. Or am I to suppose? This is when I give up.

I discover on The News that this evening Windsor castle is and has been on fire. The fire started in St George's Hall... The Queen... is Head of the Church of England... Hall... shouting at God in a hall... feeling small? it's hard... look for the purpose of the pain... who is feeling small now?... look for the will of God.

Billy is noting the names of the two halls. 'It's magic. She is an alien. Oh, no.'

Ivan is playing his Hamlet. 'To be, or not?' 'There is something rotten, in the State of Denmark.' I imagine that that must be Hamlet's mother, Gertrude; second marriage.

Remarriage... in church and the feelings this brings out... Ivan is a Roman Catholic... We approach another marriage and behold! it leaps out of existence (cf Brian Friel).

Isaiah 1
28 they that forsake the Lord shall be consumed
29 for they shall be ashamed of the oaks that ye have
desired, and ye shall be confounded for the gardens
that ye have chosen.
30 For ye shall be as an oak whose leaf fadeth, – and as
a garden that hath no water.
31 And the strong shall be as tow, and the maker of it
as a spark, and they shall both burn together, and none
shall quench them.

If this is your Will. I am privileged to serve it. I just was
trying to find out what the rules are.

There is a passage in Corinthians telling me that I may
divorce an unbeliever. My marriage was not made in a
Church. Did God bring us together? I did not divorce
Jonathan; he divorced me. Where is my sin?

Who is making these rules? God or His enemies? Did
God mean me to break my legs in daily solitary toil?

Let he, or she, who casts the first stone.

I realise that the Queen has no choices and my respect for
her increases vastly.

I have a feeling that Mark has told Abbas, Asif, a local
Muslim, and Fahruddin what is happening. Fahruddin is a
Bosnian Muslim, perhaps the first white Muslim I have met.
And I have a feeling that the Western conceptualisation of
society is coming to an end.

I had thought that I had two identities: as Linda, the
Linda I have always been, and a spiritual identity. Then I
realised that I have a unified identity, and I imagined this
creating a unity between Islam and Christianity; of a denied
self and an actualised self, of the frustrated and the fulfilled.

If only this could be communicated. I can feel the
frustration and anger of the Croats and Muslims. If we
could get this across, the war would be impossible. If we

could recreate there the understanding which we have at the multi-cultural centre.

The doors seem to swing open.

Nov. 24

Joe's birthday is going fine.

It is becoming wintry, Christmassy. Tomorrow will be the first Sunday in Advent. How long, how long? I just can't see a practical way out. Why am I attracted to cruel men? Well, you see, someone has to engage with them to get us all through. It is like a painful, icy pyramid in my side. I am standing at the gate, saying, 'Come, come'. Scott Seal, an Open Access student, agrees with me; he is more blessed in all his contradictions than others without theirs. He is a Jehovah's Witness. A pacifist. And he has been a mercenary in Croatia. Fighting out the anger he feels about his marriage. I tell him my view of the way the world is turning, telling him that I feel I must be completely mad; he, so reassuringly, says plainly, No, you are not mad.'

> 'And the Spirit and the bride say, Come. And let him that heareth say Come. And let him that is athirst come.'
> Revelation 17

There is a feeling that people are working to get me out. I am reading Revelation, Chapter 21, from verse 18. It is about the jewelled city. From the hill, a glittering city, as when I took Billy home and saw across the town. The city that disappears when you get close to it.

Nov 28th

Joe has been horribly cruel and sulky this evening. We were talking about whether the baby Jesus was just an ordinary baby; it was easier to talk as if it was just acceptably true. That he could do magic and taught people how to live and be loved by God. "Why did he have a Mummy and Daddy, then, if he was God?'

'Because he still needed someone to talk to and look after him.' (And love, I didn't say and I couldn't quite express that it is essentially human and not somehow disembodied.)

'What if there were twins. Couldn't there be two Jesuses?'

*No, because it's all to do with there only being one, special Jesus, son of one special God; you can't divide it up into parts. And God wouldn't have made two Jesuses, because He made it the way he wanted it.'

Dec 2nd

Joe is showing a horrid, stubborn rationality.

Yesterday he said categorically 'God is dead.' But I managed to move him to 'We can't actually know. I'm only a boy.' A beautiful peace suffused his face and I felt that he could think again.

This week has been rather lonely and empty, particularly today.

Dec. 4th

There goes behaviorism. There goes positivism and the requirements of verifiability. Here comes the route to feeling, the real University of life.

It is a question of being able to get to the point; the children to a church? I will do to that on Christmas Eve anyway.

The devil is sitting on my shoulder, arguing, arguing. 'I'm good, you're not. I'm not angry, you are.'

'I have never done anything wrong.'

'But have you done anything right?'

"What did you ever do to help?"

'You're unhelpable, you're beyond the pale.'

Like a spider stuck in my fallopian tubes. Tying to my eyes, my insight, my light. Oh, the spotlight on the curtain which started the fire at Windsor Castle.

'I am a little doll, with a secret.' Feed that. Joe and Henry are at home. They live here.

There is a thread, unwinding.

Driving home there is a feeling of two 'arms' not connected up, constantly wrongfooting, sticking, a gap which does not make sense. I feel a huge, powerful current of electricity – they are connected up at the highest level. Started singing. Peter. Does he realise now?

There is a fascinating article by him about Yuppies who sell water filters by pyramid selling, and whether to exploit friends financially. Of people washing out their sins. Of who is using whom. That there could exist a mutually beneficial deal.

Annabel has got her pitchfork up my bottom, to put it at its nicest. My career.

She has recently become my Line Manager and is ruling the section with a rod of irrationality. She never speaks to me and has apparently got nothing to say about education in general except on disciplinary matters.

What was the original 'beef'? That working class men have the right to have sex with every woman they want to. That women have to sleep with anyone for the cause of the working classes? I thought I had some rights, too...not to be raped.

Or defiled, abused, sickened.

Theory:

You could think of it like a sundial. I am in the centre. My partner brings out the sun (which actually shines through a connection with my energy – when Sublimation occurs?). A shadow is formed across several concentric circles.

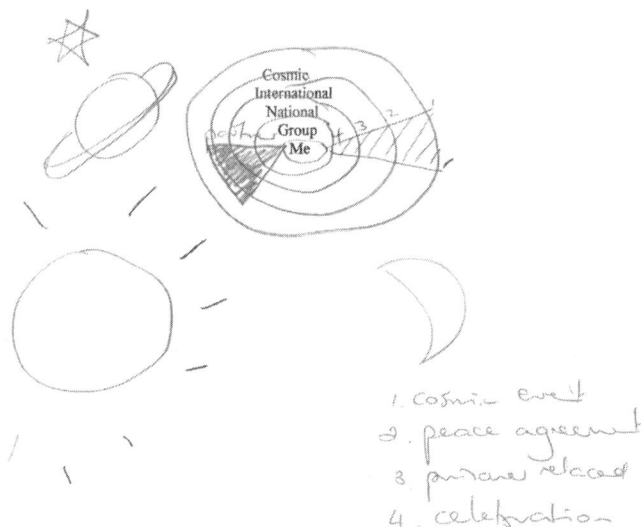

Dec. 7th

Today people are coming together. Saw Hemlata. It was lovely. She is going to a wedding. Ivan. Rema, a former student who is training to be a teacher.

Peter's Christmas card. The words came easily ('words don't come easily…like "sorry"' – Tracey Chapman) and were lively. Peter and writing. Do I send cards to my 'enemies' or not?

A peaceful weekend. A balance of the social and the spiritual. I am glad. I am so tired, stiff and unmoving at present.

Isaiah (Ivan?): 'Therefore my people shall know my name. Therefore they shall know in that day that I am he that doth speak: behold, it is I.'

7 (for Peter): 'How beautiful on the mountains are the feet of him that bringeth good tidings, that publisheth peace; that bringeth tidings of good, that publisheth salvation, that said unto Zion, "Thy God reigneth!"' Right up to the stuffed mouth, the gagged woman. 'The kings shall shut their mouths at him.' Peter, the bringer of good news. I later sang this as a hymn in Christchurch, Highbury. 'How lovely on the mountains are the feet of him, That bring good news, good news!', only to find that Peter lived around the corner.

There was an earthquake in Indonesia yesterday. I am reminded of Peter's letter, 'Kidderminster erupts' or something. What future should that little, blonde girl have had? A happy marriage. Home.

I can make my own traditions.

Out of the grave. And out comes Peter's child, a hope for all those with not only one obvious ethnicity or culture. With two or more whole ethnicities or cultures. A birth… going deeper and deeper…before time, through all time. Some people have been angry since before birth.

Dec 13th
And some take a satisfaction in driving people mad. Successfully. Horrid, envious whining, dead rats, mice, sewers. No room for anything else. I can drive people mad with just my voice. I don't want to give it up. I enjoy it, too much. The power. Fingers in my eyes, hacking away through white, chalky, sinewy stuff into GIFTS. Presents. To and from. There is some creativity and an ability to talk.

Phew.

Dec. 15th
It is Ivan on the telephone. 'Read Revelation.'

Revelation 12

5 And she brought forth a man child, who was to rule all nations with a rod of iron: and her child was caught up unto God, and to his throne.

6 And the woman fled into the wilderness, where she hath a place prepared of God, that they should feed her there a thousand two hundred and three score days.

1, 260: a place prepared by God

Gladsby Street; Dec 18th 1989 – Dec 20th 1992 = 1, 095 days plus 2 = 1.097

163 days = 6 months and 23 days is June 20th plus 23 =July 13th

And there was a war in heaven. Michael and his angels (Coventry Cathedral) fought against the dragon and the dragon fought and his angels.

Joe, there is no excuse for being rude, sucking at coconuts, me. My milk. I hate mothers.

She's a rubbish teacher, anyway. She's too soft. She's just a woman, really.

Tatty little useless old breast.

Principal: Why isn't she promotable? Dennis: (A lecturer in English now promoted over me) Well, umm…she's said to be good in bed.

My own family. The only ones who didn't stand up in the cathedral. When the soprano could not sing, for tears, 'I know that my Redeemer liveth.' Can we get out of the door without playing each other up?

Lovely carol singing.

Can you hear that moaning, damaged thing, my baby? She's got two!

She is so lucky to have a job! (but I need the money). Will anyone listen to that baby?

Christmas

Fascism.

Fascist Christmas trees fascist culture fascist baby story honk honk she isn't capable of holding down a relationship…bombs away…she's got this mad idea 'She is not a witch.'

Peter: but I would have driven you mad. Quite possibly.

But the children are more relaxed. The sun came out. Joe offered me food.

Dec. 25th

Ivan rang to tell me that his father had died, yesterday, on Christmas night. Christ is on the cross.

> How come you got everything and I got nothing?
> -Willy Russell, Blood Brothers

Ivan and I only had the right to the back route Ivan in Goldingstoke.

Me: I can't speak very easily tonight.

Ivan: Why? (Good; he asked.)

Me: Because you've taken a part of me. You need it more at the moment…but when you've finished with, can I have it back, please?

Ivan: You've taken my pain away! you're the person I pray to…God and it's taken the death of my father for me to see it.

That he'd cope, now.

Ivan's father died unexpectedly in his fifties after arriving home on Christmas Eve.

Dec. 27th

1992 was the year when Bhoutros Bhoutros Ghali was elected Secretary-General of the United Nations, January.

Three days of rioting broke out in Los Angeles, April.

The Queen addressed the European parliament for the first time since Britain joined the EU in 1973, May.

Tension increased between the USA and Iraq when the US, Britain and France established an air exclusion zone to protect the Shias. Six Tornados were sent from Britain.

The Government was criticised for the closure of coalmines, September.

The fire broke out at Windsor Castle, November.

John Major was returned to Number 10, Downing Street, and Betty Boothroyd elected first woman Speaker of the House of Commons, Neil Kinnock was replaced by John Smith.

An IRA bomb killed three people in the City of London and destroyed the Baltic Exchange.

Lloyds suffered their worst ever trading results.

Ethnic cleansing was being practised in 'Yugoslavia' and concentration camps were established.

Attempts to negotiate a democratic constitution in South Africa continued, despite massacres in Boi'patong and Ciskei.

Famine was widespread in Eastern and Southern Africa.

Formula One racing was won by Nigel Mansell...Freddie Mercury died...and Sally Gunnell and Linford Christie won gold medals in the Olympic Games in Barcelona. This was the Queen's 'annus horribilis'.

In 1993, in the Spring, an area the size of Britain was flooded in the United States. In May, Norman Lamont resigned as Chancellor of the Exchequer. Israel and the Palestine Liberation Organisation signed a peace treaty. Remember Bill Clinton's Christ-like stance? Menachem Begin would later be assassinated for his efforts.* And Bill

*   Misremembered: it was the Egyptian President Anwar Sadat, with whom Israeli Prime Minister Menachem Begin shared the 1978 Nobel Peace Prize, who was assassinated in 1981. (Another Israeli Prime Minister, Yitzhak Rabin, would be assassinated in 1995.)

Clinton... IRA bombs killed in the City of London and in Warrington – children. It was the end of any remnant of sympathy I could find for them. Serbian forces strengthened their hold on Bosnian territory and seriously wounded victims were flown from Sarajevo to Birmingham for medical assistance. The Somali Civil War continued.

The mosque in Ahodya was destroyed by Hindu extremists; Bhanumati tells me that it had been built over a Hindu temple by Hindu slave labour. Palestinian deportees spent nine months on the Israeli border. Racist grave desecration took place in Europe and there were racially motivated murders and demonstrations. Where was the post-war consensus?

Colin Jackson won his first gold medal. The Grand National was declared void. Sally Gunnell became world as well as Olympic champion.

Ivan became demanding; and eventually blackmailed me with various secrets which I did not want to hear. There were discussions about God and sexuality. He underestimated the subtlety of my views, about the sinner and the sin. God always loves the sinner. He does not love the sin. He loves Nature, in the lives of men and of women, with enough men to support, materially and emotionally, all the women. Ivan threatened me with the College authorities, the equal opportunities guidelines and so on, although these were private views, privately expressed, and I felt that he had perverted my own views of justice. He made it a battlefield, with the battalions of his local sympathisers, and I retreated. He left the following year, saying that, because he was about to become the only member of a department, he was going to better things as a head of department.

There was good work, with Inderdip and others and Joe was happy at school. Henry's teacher was convinced that he had 'problems', 'special needs', 'hearing difficulties', not addressed constructively. (Another battlefield, with me hoping for a constructive approach.)

1994

This is the year of the New Age. I see a gypsy convoy
weaving along the narrow car-lined streets. It is prophesied
that when the gypsies convert to Christianity, the New Age
will come in. This is happening. And there are corn circles
in the fields and the most imaginative Open Access group
yet. I offer to share my group with Mrs Farrah, showing
her, who has not done this sort of work before, what sort of
things can be done. Roberta Farrah is the new Open Access
manager who has taken over my work at the Multi-Cultural
Centre. She differs from me in teaching methods, taking
tape recorders for the foreign students. I do not believe they
have come from all over the world to talk to tape recorders.
To be fair, it is yet another economy in what is supposed
to be a bigger and better college. I have been praised for
this work by the Assessor; it requires organisation, tact,
creativity The students certainly show great qualities: there
is Richard, formerly a zoo-keeper, good short story writer;
Callum, from Edinburgh, full of social concern and concern
for people's rights and lifestyles. He has got that kind of
Scottish accent that could get him arrested for honesty.
And Shona, their friend, who wants to be a midwife. We are
going to have a great time and get good results. Callum's first
assignment is on travellers' rights.

We enter the realm of the slippery phrase. Lecturers are
'removed', 'packages' are arranged for them, secret deals are
struck. 'Baby Abbie comes home.' Abbie, 15 days old, was
cradled in the arms of her mother after Police found her less
than a mile away from where she had been snatched on July
1st.

Thursday 31st March

It is Maundy Thursday. The Queen is giving the Maundy money in Truro Cathedral. Tetsoya Otani is a Japanese student at the Multi-Cultural Centre. He is 19. He is in hospital with a lung infection.

The most important factor in Tetsoya's cure has been the fact that I promised him permanent security – I said always. And I remembered Hiroshima and Nagasaki. Henry was born on Hiroshima Day.

Good Friday April the First

Tetsoya has received my letter about the work he missed, apparently. One of the poems was William Blake's 'The Poison Tree'.

> I was angry with my friend
> I told my wrath, my wrath did end.
> I was angry with my foe.
> I told it not my wrath did grow

Tetsoya is good on peace and reconciliation, with that fund of goodwill one meets in young Germans, too. We are also reading a poem which tells us about the way in which peaceful overtures are misinterpreted in arguments; what does one do with the proffered olive branch? Take it? Ignore it? Misconstrue it? He understands these feelings well.

He is satisfying to teach. Tetsoya is well. And 'Yugoslavia' is at peace. By the suffering of our Lord, Jesus Christ.

April 9th

It is Vaisakhi. The decorations are up in Coventry. This festival celebrates the birthday of the tenth Guru, Gobind Singh. There is a huge BANG over Sainsbury's. A furious snowstorm breaks our overhead. It is dark with snow. Now the sun is riding high, brightly. The Grand National is about to start.

Ravinder; the new Lecturer in Politics. Possibly the first Asian lecturer to be employed by the Academic Education Department. Friend of Ivan and Gregory. He is a horse-racing fan.

He is a British Sikh.

Tuesday 10th May

This is the day on which President Nelson Mandela is inaugurated.

There is an eclipse.

I am associating this with Othello's line when he is broken in spirit at Desdemona's supposed infidelity.

'Methinks there should be eclipse of sun and moon.'

I love to know that God made the truly clever bits, too, and not just the mundane and domestic.

Eighteenth June

We go to the Moleshill Festival, the Asian community's annual fair.

I think about what Abbas said about dancing and identity; and self-respect, and being used. Then I see some Muslims, in this predominantly Sikh area. Heads are turning everywhere. What is this new movement towards a Muslim presence here? 'There are Muslims in Hedgwick Park!' I buy Henry a plastic sword and write on the scabbard:

'The pen is mightier than the sword.'

The sword is an element in the symbolic items which are carried by members of the Khalsa, the warrior movement established by this Guru.

Thursday 14 July
It is Bastille Day.

I imagine that I am presented with Callum, Ravinder and Gish, another Sikh, I think. "Choose the one who makes you smile.' I remember that a smile is a promise. I take this to be a lesson in only considering those who take one seriously.

Wednesday 13 July
I am profoundly hurt by my colleague Mrs Farrah's comment in the Open Access class last week. Teaching together, I ask to use her pen to write on the board. It is a very large whiteboard marker. 'Gosh, that's big,' I say as some sort of remark. I am devastated by her reply. 'Beggars can't be choosers,' she smugly intones in front of my class. It is the beginning of a long campaign to portray me as a single parent scrounger. A New-Age drop-out milking the College for money to raise urchins. When did I drop-out? I wonder.

All I can recall is that my husband would no longer live with his family.

Seek the will of God. This is a privilege, given for the glorification of our Lord.

'It is a privilege to teach adults,' I am just as blithely told. Indeed. And it may be a privilege to receive my teaching, too, but I do not say this.

At the end of the year, I am 'removed' from the Open Access course and I am 'removed' from the multi-cultural centre, too. But not before the course Assessor from the university delivers his report, in which my modules are singled out for special praise.

These events would appear to follow a private conversation I had with the Sikh bilingual liaison worker. I felt that she was not being used constructively; that Punjabi speakers could converse with her in Punjabi on arrival rather than be yelled at in English. It was not appreciated that most foreign students were educationally sophisticated and did not need basic Mathematics in English. Somebody must have been listening on the other side of the stock cupboard partition. 'They already know how to use a telephone,' I commented. Black looks all round. The race legislation is seen as a joke. 'We can always get rid of you' is the response. 'Shut up or ship out.' This is the first time that I have used the information that the manager laughed at someone saying that Afro-Carribeans 'all look the same' and that I'm told she said that 'It is easy to teach at the Multi-Cultural Education Centre because none of the students have got brains.'

So that was why they replaced me at The Multi-Cultural Education Centre.

1995

January

7.30ish.

At the centre of the noise, the word RESPECT jumps out – a nuclear bomb explodes – fallout – skulls, madness, paving the way for the survival of the world, after 'self'. William Blake's Self, I suppose. Twiddle, twiddle, twiddle, twit. This is supposed to be having fun? The Iraqi Revolutionary Council announce a CEASEFIRE. They will not attack anything first, as a gesture of goodwill towards Bill Clinton's administration, which begins tomorrow. The Croatians are remembering the warmth which has been ruined. This came from Mlatco admitting that he might have some idea of Russian – He can't get the articles right in English, because Serbo-Croat is like Russian, hasn't got any...

There seems to be a woodpecker with no nose painfully tapping me, the trees. 'It's boring.' 'There's no point.'

Sunday 1st February

Dreamt about Billy for the first time last night. Returning like the Prodigal Son. Today I am not well. I have a fever, swollen glands in my throat and a headache. I couldn't look at the light last night at *Romeo and Juliet* (which was lovely and sometimes very funny). What does Mlatco want when he looks straight into my eyes?

The Gregory thing with Ivan is irritating me. Gregory is a Politics lecturer and friend of Ivan and Ravinder. I am annoyed because something is being brought to my attention which is neither exciting nor interesting. There was a suggestion that I would go to a gay nightclub and I couldn't get them to see that I wouldn't get anything out of that. I worked out how they had got me into a no-win position, whereby I am a traitor if I express how I feel blackmailed.

My carrot tasted of soap! Nice, clean.

Sunday 7th February
Isn't Sunday the Sikh sabbath, too?
I am thinking of Ravinder.

> 'There exists but one God, who is called the True, the Creator, free from fear and hate, immortal, not begotten, self-existent, great and compassionate. The True was at the beginning, the True was in the distant past. The True is at the present, O Nanak, the True will also be in the future.'

Truth, not piety so much.
A morning prayer.
Joe: Where do you want to go?
Me: To the cathedral.
Henry: I don't mind if you go out. I like the places you go to.
The devil of class-mindedness.
The secret of mature belief
I have seen God. We could share the secret.
A worm through the eye sockets. Scratching away. No fly.

March 13th Saturday
Comic Relief yesterday. It was not.
Ravinder behaved as if he had never seen me before. No explanation. Perhaps because I put some money in a bucket.

I would rather be alive today than ideologically acceptable tomorrow.

200 were killed in Bombay.

Sucking away, a sweet-smelling bridge appeared out of the mud. I can feel it being constructed now. I told Ravinder and others a few weeks ago; the way of peace is beyond war.

Monday April 5th

Rain. The idea that it is not natural to want to have children will die. The harm is in the denial of nature; of the reproductive nature of sexuality. As I said to Ivan, it is profoundly anti-creative. Yesterday we attended a lovely outdoor service for Palm Sunday, shared between Holy Trinity and the Cathedral. 666 had been graffitied on the Cathedral wall. I thought of my mother's memory of her mother taking tulips to her grandfather's grave on Palm Sunday, wearing a new, brown coat, looking nice. I said to a man in the coffee queue. 'It will get worse before it gets better.'

A mouthful of holy, sweet powder.

Swallow my pride and do it the straightforward way.

The cold, chaotic barn of an unco-ordinated household. No beginnings, no endings, no privacy. Constant involvement in other people's decisions about their own comfort. No rest. No progress. This is not for me. A perpetual war-zone.

6th April

There is nowhere for the pain to go except into me. So painful. So exhausted. I appreciate the Hindus so much. They that know that God is small and needs to be consoled, comforted, fed. Hemlata, with her gifts: a sari, a mango, a pot of curry.

There's no point. No point in understanding. No light. Nose thumbed up, numb, in avoidance of the point. 'I'm not hurting you,' says the Evil One.

Wednesday 7th April

Poor little me

Stealing my strength,

Pity me,

Forever and forever.

(You will have nothing; kick).

Irritate, irritate, irritate.

I'm not jealous,

I stole everything you ever had. Pooh.

Energy utterly drained as I get out of bed.

Creativity. Reality. Covered in stinking dirt, addicted to pain. Nothing can be absorbed, digested, contained. It is just fired back.

I miss Ravinder – who knows why now? I imagine that he is looking out to sea, off Gran Canaria. He is on holiday.

Let go. Leave that space for me to breathe.

'She isn't on the list of the official oppressed, so we do not have to do anything.' There is no such thing as need; a tiny, occasional helping hand that would set a huge, virtuous circle in motion. 'Do it all yourself.'

The Devil plays God, but in the form of a person, not a God. He teaches the believer how to please God, but does not believe. You see, Christ takes away all pain, even the pain of the divorced and he does not send anything he does not mean us to benefit from. Finally, he has no interest in petty blame. 'Om.'

Enlightenment; one's head pops out and all is clear. It can all be viewed as a means to some end one can understand.

Ivan, you knew who I was and you persecuted me.

YOU ARE NOT ALLOWED TO HURT ME.

Pain does not ennoble the one who inflicts it or the victim. It lowers everyone.

A hook suspends me while a ball-pane hammer knocks away at my satisfaction, icelike. 'We may not know, we cannot tell, what pain he had to bear.'

Horrid devil-face with tongue stuck up and thumbs to temples, waggling its fingers. Splitting everyone down the middle. And finally... a revolting load of vegetables!

They are snatching each breath in impossibly tense voices. 'Life at crisis-point,' I thought and one small moment of peace, space was created between the prongs of that noise which I can breathe in, thank the Lord.

April 8th

I am breaking down the wall of 'knowing' disbelief 'it cannot be' weak spider-like legs dangling from their painful hook which is clamped onto His breath.

I can feel Ravinder's warmth. 'I'm known as Pete actually.' With all the work I've done on the names of people from various cultures, I cannot bring myself to call him Pete. I think he has been used.

Good Friday

An ice and metal hook is destroying the breath. This is containable because it is so clearly pure pain, now.

Let me walk out: go forth into the world in peace. Phew. Fangs into each eye, consonant. Ultimately painful. The middle way utterly ruined.

'But all she wants is a nice man.'

The smashed container, defiled and destroyed. 'The dream Tito had of Yugoslavia.'

The weak will smash it… horrible, strong, alive, bee buzzing around and projecting pain, into the most sensitive parts of people, automatically and without compunction.

'This isn't really happening.' 'We haven't really ripped the… out of you.'

The key.

Fairy stories.

'I couldn't even imagine… God.' Oh God, I've just been sitting there all my life waiting for Him to be true.

A battle over the existence of God; as it affects behaviour, not just whether it is the case that God exists or not. Whether there is anything of inherent value (even you?).

Strong, orange, (marry) taste released.

Envy of youth, life, joy.

Oh Ivan, take me down from here.

'Oh Lord, remember me
When you come into your kingdom
Oh Lord, remember me
When you come into your kingdom.'

Good lunch – lamb, grapes, crackers, tea.

Can I let the church feed me (communion?)?

Asleep this afternoon. Waking, I feel that a large burden has been lifted from me as I become emotionally detached from the Cathedral. How it has become almost everything right. Its care, its love, its carefulness with what has been presented by the twentieth century and its respect for the spirit of Christ. Though Mothering Sunday wasn't a mothering Sunday, really, with Joe and Henry at Jonathan's – all the children gave their mothers bunches of flowers. I am ready to turn outward. I must remember to take the church with me. Including the Catholic Church.

Friday April 16th

Srebrenica. Confused about God's motives and sympathies. Easier to think of Peter's Last Battle, Armageddon, the overall plan.

At the end of the tunnel is knowledge about the mind of God. Is the discovery of an ancient mystery.

'Srebrenica is about to fall.' Will the Muslims be forced to convert to Christianity? Because I love you. Otherwise I will always be terrorised by men. We are a family, because we love God.

Peter's Last Battle. Without Christ, we are nothing/ God wants peace with justice and a χChristian future safe for Christ, who wants peace. Peter writes to me in November. 'I am thinking of converting to BCP Christianity.'

Sunday April 18th

Low-spirited, I didn't feel like going to the Cathedral and felt exposed. I think they realise. Everything was expressed that way and there was nothing to contradict this. I felt very shy and moved. Just don't say anything to me. It was beautiful.

Came home. Didn't want to be known. There was a sermon about the disciples being afraid. The Jews. The Authorities.

I remembered how Marion Fry had emphasised the unity of the Trinity. 'Those who have seen me have seen the Father.' The Mother. I have been here for all time.

April 24th

There was one, rotten black one in the children's crisps. We threw it away. Reward the Christian world. Can you have God without Christ? There are Indian Christians, culturally

Indian. St Thomas converted India, arriving at Goa. I decided to renounce the men in the Staff Room again and felt much better. Leyland Daf jobs have been secured.

Sunday April 25th

I don't have to do anything. It is about peace. Leave it in the hands of God. Renewing a broken world… the former things will pass away.

> Oh Lord, remember me
> When you come into your kingdom
> Oh Lord, remember me
> When you come into your kingdom

April 26th

I heard a man laugh last night. Vomiting all milk out with razor blades, razor blades in the stem of the brain and no milk can get through, razor blades instead of sibling rivalry.

No thought.

29th April

Pull the whole thing out; not just the umbilical cord, but the placenta as well!

It was a poison placenta. Good and bad placenta. How could we ever have survived?

My God; and it was so strong.

Three Bosnian Muslims arrived today, browny, greeny, greyey, poor.

Faffing around with my insides – the opening is the opening of the umbilical cord, with evil, pain, broken glass shoved into the end of it and checking that I am not too sure about what is going on. 'Ah – the sexual organs are connected to the reproductive system – I hadn't thought of that.'

It is my body. It is where I live. And you cannot do that without involving my head, too. Emptying, abortion, split from the revulsion of thinking about consequences. 'Thou shalt bring forth thy children in sorrow… and thy days shall be numbered.' (Are you sure? Do you really mean that one?)

Saturday May 1st

The sun is shining and I feel happier about the Cathedral. Depression and the attacks of winter have been fading. Put flowers in my hair. Be a May queen. The fulfilment of Blake's vision. Jerusalem in Albion. Rebuild Jerusalem.

I wanted Ivan to understand that the fight to be mother is important to a woman. The mother is the centre of everything. Yes, I know he adores his mother. As I write, a huge thunderclap bursts, or is it a warehouse collapsing on the industrial estate? A light like an arc lamp shines, as if a brilliant lamp has been ignited in the uppermost parts of the universe.

'Maybe she is not a cliché. Maybe she is leading the Zeitgeist, not following it.' We do not worship the God of instant ritual without feeling, with no soul. Cup Final.

– Norman Lamont was sacked as Chancellor of the Exchequer on this day.

He looked defensive and insecure. The cartoon was about Freud, and then about Lawrence.

Tuesday 19 June

– Feeling terrible. Hardly move.

'Society'. Parents – they are still young! Phew – I feel better. Well. Home. Settling. Egg… on face. 'But I've always treated you like a Bimbo… winked at you. I thought you were a tragic failure.' 'You can't learn us anything.'

As I leave the multi-cultural centre, the newspaper tells of the incredible rescue of 365 hostages in a hijack in Japan – 22nd June. I say goodbye to Tetsoya. He is returning to Japan to train in the leather industry. I hear him talk to another Japanese student and can't believe how beautifully he speaks Japanese. I tell him that he can rely on me. Always.

On the twenty-third, we are given John Major's famous challenge to his party: Put up or shut up.' ('Major gambles and provokes leadership battle'). My sentiments, about a lot of things.

A week later the *Independent* has a report of a split in the Serb leadership, a development I would think one would welcome in terms of weakening their solidarity.

The Tories are urged to unite against John Major. My old boyfriend Nick reports on improvement in the pension rights of divorcees. The temperature in Herne Hill reaches 32 degrees Centigrade. I wonder how I can tell the British people that if we are to protect our climate, we must become a little bit more depressed.

4th July

– Jana Novotna cried when she lost (didn't win) Wimbledon. The Duchess of Kent put her arm around her.

Depressive functioning is breaking out all over. No-one even wanted it to be true.

I am made to undertake that I will not talk about racism at work. Even though my job is to implement the language policy as part of the Equal Opportunities procedures. I can't believe that this can really be enforced. 'We will prosecute you for slander.' 'They are afraid at the Multi-Cultural Centre that you are going to come back and kill them'!

8 July

On the eighth of July, Peter writes in the magazine at the weekend. The article is about night doctors on call. It seems that hysteria is powered by a wish to be visited by someone who will cure one in the night. I am reminded of this, and pleased by his sympathy with people who are at times at the mercy of these fantasies.

Saturday 10th July

Tension built up and was released. I realised, felt, that there would no longer be a nuclear war. We went to a cricket match in Edgbaston, Birmingham. Afterwards, we walked in Cannon Hill Park. Droplets of rain were hanging in the sunshine, but never where we were. Just a few Muslims saw this; no-one else was there. It was a match; the word used for a marriage arrangement. On the way home, we turned left at the crossroads in Meriden, this being the centre of England, and noticed the right-hand foot of a rainbow. A sunbow, I thought, which Joe showed me. This was the home of the woman who was murdered in this town, or more correctly, at home, by her husband. He broke into the building society where she worked, stole some money, then dumped her body near here, making it look as if she had been killed at work. Her husband was found to have killed her and then tied himself up in a rope. Thus the police found him the following morning, saying that he had been attacked by intruders. I could see parallels here... And when released by police from the rope, he did not go to the bathroom – he had not, in fact, been tied up all night.

16th July

It seems people become very stuck or schizophrenic because they cannot trust their attachments (sneeze sneeze), there are too many of them, they are too split, there is not a strong enough I.

I am thinking of Dennis, the man who took over my life at work, imagining, 'Do you know, you were right about discrimination? You could have continued to talk about it for ever and I would never have given you any credit for it.' There was a huge thunderclap. I write this while the rain has stilled. And now the rain is torrential. No, I see what you mean. The earth pulsates to the beat of your body.

One senses God's fury. YOU TAINTED A WOMAN WHO WAS ONCE PURE. I wonder if Ravinder realises that we have both been abused. Perhaps the missing piece is the idea that Alan was supposed to have been put at risk at catching AIDS from me! This part of the story had been communicated in all seriousness to the college where I worked, being construed as providing evidence of my poor character and lack of consideration for the health of others; and taken seriously, though I denied it. It was evidence to allege. It was not evidence to deny. Small chance of AIDS, in fact. No chance. My doctor could have refuted this. So could Jonathan and Daniel, my only partners in the fifteen years since catching AIDS had become at all possible. And here I was, in rude good health. But reason did not prevail. 'It counts against her, with the other proofs.' The risks to my job were increasing.

I found it too far-fetched to talk about it.

I felt they were using Ravinder to defeat me, as if he were a racial representative and not his own man. Another factor in the Othello syndrome.

Ivan is in Chicago. The Mississippi is sixteen miles wide. It has rained since April.

Let my people go.

'She is the third planet from the sun. She has a sister, who is the nearest, who is called Mercury and a brother, who is Love.' Isn't that one female?

Ask Dom. It's called the dance of the spheres.

21st July

I wrote to Tony Unwin, my Greek god at eighteen. Karyn Smith and Claire(?) Cahill were released from prison in Singapore. They seem to be particularly devalued, being girls associated with drugs; but one cannot be too approving, either. I re-read Tony's letters to me. One from a lodging house in Kathmandu, complaining of a large, empty bed. I never knew whether this was a cry of loneliness or a request for me to take the next plane. Something I could not have afforded, anyway. I was cheered by thinking of what could have been. Suffolk farmer's wife scenario.

22nd July

God is indivisible; and not particular to particular religions. Jesus Christ is Lord of All.

Does that go with the idea of the Trinity? I suppose it could do.

I suppose it would mean that the other religions have not got all the elements of the Trinity.

One is upside down screaming while the others have their elbow in one's mouth. Held in the grinding, crashing red-raw womb of the universe, impaled on a pencil. The breath ripped out from the back of the nose, a pain-wracked red-raw me.

'I gave you this and you turned it to shreds, raw in its
pain, the essentials so abused and battled over.
As many times as I have died for you you will die for
me.
Give up your blasphemy and humiliation and
remember the home.
Put your head before your pleasure and repent.
Repent. Repent. You will be saved.
But when, when?
When you have ears to hear and eyes to see.'

It seems that we have to learn the lessons of the
Reformation. And Cambridge, being a home of the
Reformation, is always a good place to start.

Holidays.

23rd August

Food reaches Mostar, Bosnia-Herzegovina. There is a small
ancient bridge there ('most'). I associate this with the little
bridge across the river Cam at King's College, which was
built to replace the colonnade which ran across King's
lawn, over the river and into the earth abutment in the cow
pasture – Medical aid has reached them. I can feel the peace
– a fluttery, fizzy, beauteous amazement. It is not boring. It
is not an absence of anything; war, struggle, significance. It is
a presence.

> (Be still, for the presence of the Lord
> Is moving in this place.)

I think of the Cathedral, hoping that they feel it there. I
visit King's College chapel, which is now worried, aware,
commercial where it had once been warm, tolerant, with a
good-humoured welcome. The voices are still wonderful.

Spoken and sung. And nothing else exists. *Kyrie. Kyrie eleison.* This is where I come from; this is who I am. No arguments about personal politics here, or not in public at least. I grew up here, queuing around the court, laughing in the congregation, trying not to cough during the broadcast. It is the great generosity of Cambridge. This is my freedom; I can sing like a King's boy and sleep through the organ recital.

Wednesday 25th. August

Back home, though there often seems to be more than one home, I hear Colin Semper *'Semper sempitorum requiem'* – reading on the radio: 'For the marriage of the Lamb is come (and the bride has made herself ready for him).'

Monday 13th September

Israel: P.L.O.

I read the penultimate chapter of Revelation in bed – Jerusalem.

Nine o'clock news: Jerusalem. Does not belong to any one religion. It is important to Christians, too.

This is an unusual mention of the meaning of Jerusalem for Christians, I feel, and not only for Jews; or Arabs. Meaning. We have jettisoned the meaning of meaning in Cambridge. We cannot afford to do so.

Jerusalem will have to be shared.

Tuesday 14th September

A mind of my own and physical strength. This is what the Devil is rammed up into, playing with fire.

Wednesday 15th September

How can you kill them when you don't even know who they are when you meet them?

It's totally random! And you think it's justice! You said I was working class because I live in Gladsby Street. What am I? Would you want me on your side or not? Asian people, are they fascists or working class? You're only interested in them if they give up their culture and join in with you. Is that Working Class? My family had a culture and some worked in the coalmines. Aren't we always just talking about your image of the white locals?

The nurseries even bombed the children's names.

The baby actually has a home.

Those children went out shopping, just like anyone would.

And I am not just a figure at work.

'When she goes home, she is on her own.'

Women's domestic oppression. 'If she died, no-one would know.' Are the men abused in their own homes? Whatever colour they are.

Who really cares about women's lives?

Who really cares for 'other people', as people? Christ.

They had ignored our bodies, our menstruation, pregnancy, childbirth. The only women who progressed had to pretend they had not got children. How was that progress?

Their politics was about what was on television.

Right at the root of that noise is my soul.

Catch my soul.

Follow me, follow me.

1996

March 3rd

The circle is made. And what is it, so defiled, kicked? It is the crescent moon. It is the moon which denotes the peace of Islam. With a dove cooing. It is the Indian night; the moon which hangs over the Taj Mahal. It is the Japanese night, with the caged nightingale and its songs. From West to East – Allah. Justice and mercy be with you. Peace be with you. The peace of God be with you.

Shalom.

It is not a trap.

December 25th

The Queen reminds us of Christ's words and we know what gives her strength:

> 'I was in the world
> And you knew me not.'

It is not very long since 1996. Eternal youth: you reach the point of genital injury and become able to refresh yourself, perpetually. Constant renewal, drinking the liquid which perpetually cascades, thinking 'What is God's will?' Ah! ... Then the body renews and you are defended from danger; you are spotting the hazards and negotiating them, swallowing pain, saying 'Show Me the Way'.

I wanted to steal something from you that was very very close to you, that was culturally the very stuff of you; your father, your nearest friend, the most beloved boss' most pretty daughter.

No, I don't miss you; I have got what is you here and you haven't got it any more. I can make you so jealous it pares you to the bone.

February 14th – St Valentine's Day

Peter seems to inform me that he will get sufficiently high up to see if he can do anything about Rushdie. Between us, see if we can't arrange something. 'Right.' Rushdie has got to apologise and Iran has got to elect a more democratic government. I would like us to agree on Thou Shalt Not Kill, at least.

Monday 19th February

It is Callum's birthday. He is about to take his exams. It is Daniel's birthday.

It is three years since Ravinder and I showed signs of mutual attraction and nothing has happened. Callum asks me out to lunch.

Andrew arrives, a teaching student. Seems interesting – very attractive – has been a magician and circus artist, visited India, looked at the patterns of things, is obviously bright and does not respect Christians. He has already managed to land a job ideally placed next to xxxx Cathedral and a mile or so from where Jonathan lives. Very promising, if a little young.

It is Eid, the end of Ramadan.

And on Tuesday it is Pancake Day.

It is April 3rd, the third day in Holy Week.

There is brilliant sunshine, the atmosphere one of 'war is over' And the lamb will lie down with the lion. Something about the cockatrice's den…

Andrew teaches *The Royal Hunt of the Sun*, by Peter Shaffer (rather lives up to the dislike of Christians theme, though the Sun God is perhaps a step on the way) 'The eagle eats the condor, the condor eats the crow, and they would eat all the birds in the sky'. A question of who will eat whom. As if knowledge could be achieved by ratiocination or wishful thinking.

April 5th-7th

I visit Norwich Cathedral. It is its 900th anniversary. The Queen has just distributed the Maundy money here. I watch a mystery play in the cloisters and attend the Easter Sunday service; a very full church, it is difficult to find anywhere to sit. I am joined by a smelly tramp who shouts insults at the church in general and the clergy in particular then sings like a chorister, knowing all the words by heart. It looks as if he spends his Easter processing from one ecclesiastical establishment to the next.

April 23rd

A major poet visits the college to read some of her poems and is addressed by her Christian name only and treated like a schoolgirl; a strengthening experience. I am not the only person addressed like the girl next door.

Saturday 26th April

I see Terry Waite in a newsagent's in Cambridge. I would love to say something to him,

I am not close enough to say hello.

There is a ceasefire in the Lebanon.

An agreement between Israel, the Lebanon, Hezbollah, I think, brokered by the United States.

11th May

We go to hear Verdi's Requiem in Coventry Cathedral. Rosemary sings in the choir. We sit on the front seats regaled by the soloists and Joe follows all the words in Latin. 'Hear that anger…feel that anger…' I think to myself in the *Dies Irae*, 'That is how it will be.'

Monday 17th June

I only died for the Muslims, the Christians. I was crucified for the Sikhs.

Ravinder takes me to a meeting with the Personnel Officer in which I am reprimanded for mentioning my knickers. 'And if I mentioned my knickers would you think it was acceptable?' roars the male Personnel Officer. 'Well, yes, if it was tastefully done and…'

Tuesday June 2

A feeling of relaxation over racialism. I could feel it at the school. There was a real joy about the Asian people. I sent a Study Support Helpline sticker to Calum, but, he is gone. His relationship with Jenny has collapsed, ours hasn't got off the ground because of practical hesitations and misunderstandings and he is off back to Scotland, his qualifications, which would have been excellent, incomplete. A real waste. How far was he the unwilling adjudicator of an undeclared war between myself and Mrs Farrah? 'A non-finisher,' I say to myself, but I can feel the blame hanging in the air about me.

Well, there might have been problems, I console myself. I had asked him to Gujarati classes and he had shown no interest, even in the idea. I had talked about Wales and all he had wanted was Jenny's native Shropshire.

Saturday 20th July

We repair to the Isle of Mull for two weeks, visiting castles, having picnics and watching the Olympic Games on the little portable television.

I find a verse on the wall at Torosay Castle: 'It rained and rained and rained and rained / The average was well maintained', and indeed it did, for three days, constantly. Returning from Tobermory one afternoon, I mentally compose a postcard to Andrew and as I think of the words a rainbow forms, a perfect arch across the Sound of Mull from the little island station to the mainland. Two legs, then another whole rainbow. It is a very high tide.

We send a postcard to Joe's Muslim friend from Iona. The sky is as blue and the water as clear as that of a Greek island; but cold. I feel a deep, warm heat as we write; 'She knows about us. She is here for all of us, not just the Hindus. To avenge the death of Jesus Christ. The Muslims did not put Christ on the cross.'

I read Peter's obituary of his father in the newspaper. He was a Second World War poet and Spitfire pilot. His father looks interesting – not too formal. He was married five times; this gives me a little more insight into Peter's marital feelings. So what had happened to his mother, the kind lady who had introduced us?

Wednesday 25th September

I come in the name of the LORD.

'And in the evening, Jesus took bread and broke it, saying 'Eat, drink, do this in remembrance of me', says the Eucharistic prayer.

I am thinking of the clergy at the Cathedral: John Petty, Michael Sadgrove, Paul Oestreicher.

Barrie Hinksman, a former therapist of mine. I saw him on Easter Saturday last year, when we wrote letters for Amnesty International and his eyes were failing. What couldn't he see?

Wise men.

Sunday 29th September

Thirty-five years of *Songs of Praise*! A wonderful Gospel choir sang. These are not 'Blacks', not 'a black choir', they are people. The audience was in tears, crying for the black people of Birmingham, in conjunction with the clergy at Coventry Cathedral, St Michael, and all his angels. 'Give thanks', they sang.

October

Our youngest cat's leg is smashed. Joe notices and we take her straight to the vet. Her pelvis might be damaged, too. The lady in front of us in the queue has a nice, long chat with her friend, the receptionist, especially prolonged to teach us our manners.

The cat has recovered by Christmas.

31st October

We read Shylock's 'And spurn me as you would a stranger cur / Over your threshold.'

Kicked like a dog. And my feelings about Shylock, about Wales, about ethnicity, all come together. The aim is to restore my father as the rightful King of Briton. Cymbeline.

Shakespearean themes.

Saturday 9th November

It is Remembrance Sunday and it is Diwali.

11th November

The anniversary of the birth/death of Marie Curie, killed by her own experiment. 1867-1934.

I am teaching Teresa, brilliant Polish pharmacologist. Her work is on depression. My work is against depression.

November 13th

'I am trying to get you to see. People tell lies. People need protection from them.' How do I feel? Like a wet rag. Droopy, tired legs, no stuffing, floppy hair. Your impotent self, I presume.

Friday 29th November

A weeping painting is featured in the *Independent*. The painting is called 'the olive twig spurned.'

I am in touch with Alex again, saintly former boyfriend from university. He and his wife have lost a child. I find her again in a fuchsia from Repton, Peter's father's old school.

'? (the usurpers) will give up the throne of David.' And a golden glow spreads through King's, through my face, through a powerful Turner sky and the rain stops. The rightful authorities will be returned.

Wednesday 4th December

I return from London on Y Ddraig Cymraeg, the Welsh dragon.

19 December

For Christmas, Bob tells me about 'the Congs', the
Congregationalists, and my search for my roots is complete.
Bob Sloan is a mature student on the Literature for Pleasure
course, a humorous writer. We are Welsh Independents. The
Calvinists who kept the faith, in the ten commandments,
in the revealed word of God, in the promise of ages. I know
why I love this community of Muslims, who, of course, do
not drink alcohol. They are the Eastern brothers and sisters
of my own church chosen ones.

> Over... of wind and sky
> I have heard my people cry
> Here I am Lord.

Andrew has left. He has been told lies, it seems, and
manipulated and used, in an ostentatious pose of power and
of control, communicative relationship rendered impossible.
I see him again once – in Toys 'R' Us.
    Tears.
    Relationship whole and relationship broken.
    The circle of life: friendship renewed, friends returning.
    The impulse towards conclusion. The longing for peace.

1997

January 19th

My spirit was at How End, in the garden, dead, murdered, all this time. Twenty years. The baby Alex lost was the baby we did not have, a baby encapsulated in a fuchsia. Fuchsias for the future. 'Last night, I dreamed I went to How End again.' We need to re-connect sexuality with babies. Our spirits were locked together there. Let those whom God has brought together...

The Election

Blair is to play Jesus Christ. It is the ending of *Macbeth*. Malcolm returns, with his troops, the Usurper's head on a platter. Did you not know the price of peace?

Rivers was cold and handsome. Alex' wife is mad, so he says, and we do have some wonderful conversations, and he is not handsome any more, but I do not want to marry him.

March First. St David's Day

She looks Welsh; they've got their own. 'Welsh Christianity is the sensuous expression of the gifts of God.' P. Crowse.

March

I notice colours. Orange; a poem by Sheila Dunne. Blue: a piece of writing by Shirley, Indigo, a tango, Red; it is read, Violet; the flowers, the African violet, a gift.

Sunday July 6th

Uncle Ben was born 100 years ago today.

He was a Deacon in the chapel, a respectable 'working class' man.

O Iesu mawr… Oh great Jesus…

Come, oh Lord Jesus, come.

July 11th

The magnificent seven come riding over the hill: Paul, Simon. Martin, Dave Grey, Andrew, Francis, Daniel. Then there is the prophet Jeremiah, who writes in the first person, or the false prophet, who apes him. I think they are both J. That is, Josh Moonshine, my partner in 1998.

Paul is a film-maker who appreciates creativity. Simon, the studio technician, similar. Martin a lovely hairdresser, represents beauty. Francis, my old, old sparring partner, friend.

I realise that the Welsh won the Battle of Bosworth Field, which is just a few miles away from here. We visit it from time to time, walking about the fields, trying to work out the course of the battle. I cannot make the point that England lost. There is an argument in the café. The children are becoming impatient with me and I can't explain that I'm not consciously doing anything to be difficult. A nation united under the Tudors. 'We have remembered our history. You have forgotten yours.'

This is a quotation from a short story by Arthur C. Clarke. The last line is 'If you are still white, we can cure you.'

Render unto no man evil for evil.

Friday July 18th

A ceasefire is predicted in Ireland. This is to reward Mo Mowlem for the manner of her treatment by the press during the election campaign. Prince Charles is bringing home the future Queen of England? It is her 50th birthday. Jonathan is learning something about my authority in parenting.

Prepare ye the way of the Lord.

July 20th

I have rights in my own home and authority over the children. It is as if I must bow to Jonathan's authority.

Twelve o'clock today – the IRA ceasefire is announced. I am in Great St Mary's, which is the University church of Cambridge.

But do the English Protestants support the Irish Protestants?

Aren't the Calvinists on their own?

I went to visit the United Reformed Church for the first time. Emmanuel. God is with us.

It is quiet. All quiet. Be still and know that I am Lord. Equal rights. Minority rights.

Women's rights.

Later, I am remembering a conversation with Daniel in Hyde Park.

Me: But there – is also a poetic view of the universe – the sun goes up, the sun goes down – which is also true. The geocentric view, not just the scientific one.

Daniel, who is a scientist: No, those things just aren't true...

Evening – Prepare ye the way of the Lord
(Refrain, from *Godspell.*)

Wales – the chapel – the elders.

A'r glwyd dyma fi
Ar dy alwad di
Canna feinaid yn y gwaed
A gaed a'r Galfari
I am coming, Lord
At your call
My being is in the blood
On the land at Calvary

I hear a story from Swansea URC. No, I said a paraclete, not a parakeet. I will send you a paraclete; I will send you an advocate and a comforter.

I am the Comforter, come alive.

Saturday 26th July

We celebrate fifty years of India's independence. Nehru? Mahatma Gandhi, his Christ-like example of passive resistance. His influence. No war is just. It cannot have just results. Reward the Hindus for their pacifism with gifts.

Nehru said, 'We have a tryst with destiny'.

Independence and the Welsh. Fireworks.

Today we celebrate our Independence Day.

'I am old, Peter. Ever so much older than twenty,' says Wendy from the nursery.

I grow old. I grow old. I shall wear the bottom of my trousers rolled. Suffer the little children... Melanie Klein was celibate too.

Friday First August

The Song of the Fates? by Brahms. Sviatoslav Richter is dead. The Prom is beautiful.

On the Sunday, I hear a little song which goes like this: 'I may never walk with the infantry, ride with the cavalry, I shoot with the artillery, I may never suit with the enemy, for I'm in the Lord's Army.' It is the Salvation Army, beloved of my grandmother, who would always give them ten shillings at Christmas.

John Calvin believed in the primacy of the scriptures in matters of faith and in the predestination of God's elect.

Tuesday 5th August

I had a dream towards morning that I met Ruth and Steve and said 'Hello' and put my arms around them, and they showed me Rebecca, who was lively and healthy. And some cheese, which Ruth had bought for her.

And from the chorus? Student Ashley cries 'Preach it. To be apart from you is death.' Ashley so naturally wanted to know if Jesus was true or not; this, a six-foot-two gangly youth with hair like an American Indian's. And Ajay and Kev. And Rich; all hovering around six foot. Utterly harmless. Huge. 'If anyone attacks us with a machete, we'll just stick Age in the doorway.'

Recurrent theme: Preach it! (from 'I Know Why the Caged Bird Sings')

My friend Ruth, Steve, J. and I hold up the four corners of the Earth, a world free from evil, from disease, from hatred and racism and intimidation. Four points of the compass. Four winds. Four Gospels – or more?

We have suffered, oh we have suffered.
How long, oh Lord, how long? Oh Israel.
How long, oh Lord, how long?
To be apart from you is death.
I want to cross over
I want to cross over
I want to cross over into
Camp ground

And when it was evening, Jesus took bread and it broke, so he fixed it.

Sunday August 16th

Tension, heat.
    Heard, sung 'Agnus dei, agnus dei':

> Qui tollis peccata mundi
> Dona eis requiem
> Agnus dei Agnus dei

A kind of call from a far and kind place; past Lancaster and superstition and witchcraft, and witch hunts.
    On Sunday, the War Requiem is sung at the Proms.

> Dona nobis pacem
> Dona nobis requiem

Alex. His subject, Latin.

Friday 31st October

Happy Diwali! Shoob Diwali! Diwali Mubarak!

I come as a thief in the night.

It is night. It is night and there is a little light shining. A star. It is night and the men are coming; watching the star, they process through the night. I come, I come, as a thief in the night. The witches are dying. The witches are dead. These people aren't the pagans.

They have their own ways. Rama has been sent into exile and had to leave his beloved Sita. After fourteen years, he finds his way home to her, guided by many little lights, little lit wicks which float in small dishes. Or for the Sikhs, it commemorates the Holy Golden Temple at Amritsar Candles stand in halved onions. *Bydd goleini yn yr hwyr.*

There will be light at eventide – a promise my mother made me.

November 8th

We go to the chapel in Tamworth castle. This castle fought away the Norsemen. This Northernmost fortification is perched just on the A5, Watling Street, which marked the border between the Norse lands and the Saxons. The ghost of St Editha of Polesworth hectors a chap, who looks just like Alan, bolt upright in his bed. Her voice rings out 'Repent, repent.' He has ransacked the Abbey and routed the nuns. But then we pass into the chapel (Protestant) and the peace sings.

She is with me for nights. Tormented, insistent.

And Princess Diana is here, too, most warm, most cold.

> The seas shall waste, the skies in smoke decay
> Rocks full to dust and mountains melt away
> But fix'd his word, His saving power remains
> Thy realm forever lasts, Thy own Messiah reigns

This is embroidered on a sampler there.

Where is the bridge between Christianity and Islam? Is Mohamed (p.b.u.h.) the prophet and interpreter of Jesus Christ? Is the bridge illusory? An ideal of perfect love?

J. thinks I should compromise with his lack of faith. I try to explain that I really believe what I believe.

November 13th

'I am trying to get you to see. People tell lies. People need protection.'

How do I feel? Like a wet rag. Droopy, tired legs, no stuffing, floppy hair. Your impotent self, I presume.

December 19th

There have been natural disasters across the globe. Belatedly, the UN forces arrive in East Timor and we are so glad.

Pete's son has died in a car crash on the A5. Peter Manson is a lecturer and former Mayor of North Warwickshire. I see them as Old and Siward. Old Siward mourns the utter waste and the utter necessity. And Jackie is dead. She died in Coventry, a plastic bag over her face. She was my sister's friend, mentally ill, poor, bringing up two sons. J. tells me blithely that he does not want our children.

St John Rivers was cold handsome and she 'spurned his counterfeit idea of love.' Alex' wife is mad, so he says, and we do have some wonderful conversations, and he is not handsome, but I do not want to marry him.

There is one who qualifies for the Mr Rochester candidature, but he is far away and has rejected me most categorically.

1998

There are only two years to go now. No-one wants to pay for the Gallery of the Spirit at the Millennium Dome. This speaks a lot to me. No-one wants to pay. 'It is free,' I seem to hear them say, but it is not free. It is expensive, unique, utterly precious. 'The poor are with you always.' I need a living wage, for wear and tear and opportunities foregone and because love is not copious or spoiling, though it is always. I cannot work here while I am loving there. Christ did not make a virtue of poverty, he made a sin of it, but He taught us that if we wish to follow His example we must be prepared to suffer with Him, and that in doing this, God will provide. He loved the poor. He was Lord of all.

February

The students are very frightened. They fear a war with Iraq. Saddam Hussein must allow the United Nations to inspect their weapons sites. But along with this, or just before, an American President is shuffling out of his relationship with a young woman who worked at The White House. And the theme of our concerns is, rather, male responsibility, and the corruption which accompanies irresponsibility.

March

I start learning Welsh. I found the grave of Wittgenstein and placed a flower on it. He knew what language could teach us about thought and knew that introspection on its own does not reveal very much except what happens when we introspect, as I had said at the beginning, in Oxford. It was like death. The link with language and how language is used. It was a Jew who showed us the way out of the wilderness, real empiricism?

Or is Blair Malcolm from *Macbeth*? Is it Jane Eyre? J.'s like Mr, Rochester. But Mr Rochester was not handsome. Easter warms my feet.

Jonathan returns from Sri Lanka.

Good Friday

A disaster movie. We are en route for Cambridge. We hear that Warwickshire is flooding and think we will be all right, but Huntingdonshire is one foot deep in water. In all directions. I am afraid that I will meet a dinosaur along the next country lane we attempt.

We have to turn back to a roadside hotel. *Jumanji* on the television and Easter eggs. The proprietor of the service station gives out free coffee. At three o'clock. This is Good Friday. We continue four hours later, arriving in Cambridge to view wet but game politicians announce the Good Friday Agreement, a proposed peace for Ireland.

Easter itself is wonderful musically, with a string quartet in King's, but as damp spiritually as the fens outside.

Easter

Peace is coming, peace is coming. The noise is lessening. Christ is risen.

Channel 5 begins, with a programme about Mr Blair at Oxford, and some Broad Left chums.

Easter Sunday, in King's. It was Simon Peter who came to the tomb, with Mary Magdalene, I realise, and Peter the journalist warms my feet.

Friday 22nd May

A vote on the Good Friday Agreement.

Repent. Repent. Repent. There will be no forgiveness without repentance (or only a bit, anyway.) You only made me ill in The Gulf. You tore me to shreds in Ireland. What are you doing, breaking me in two? The Welsh Protestants held me for all these years. They did not kill anyone.

Seek only the will of God. How dare you question this?

Well, I suppose they are only talking about somewhere to talk.

First June

Xantippe threw a glass of wine over Socrates, when he claimed that women are irrational.

What is ironic about this? It was a rational act.

Glenn Hoddle, the Christian football manager, wrings a real apology out of a player who has stayed out all night the night before the World Cup begins; apologises to his wife, his children, the British public, the other players. We see what an apology can be.

While I am ill, somebody makes up 10 'complaints' about my work. After I had complained about a few students' behaviour (I have 160 this year), when I told them that my family was Welsh; sheep noises, cartoon sheep drawn on the blackboard, a toy sheep which made 'baa-ing' noises set off when I was teaching. For months. A 'Hearing' follows the 'complaints'. 'She has a florid personality.' (Do you mean torrid?) I would like to tell them about Mrs Rochester, the displaced wife, but am hardly allowed to speak. There is no evidence against me. Only the word of a few embittered colleagues. I have to resign.

They do not know anything about the transference and projection and to mention these would bring about ridicule and 'You can't bring that in here!'

So how shall I leave all this? Give them some worthy advice and the forty or so complaints I have amassed myself and been too afraid to tender. A list of the more criminal activities for the police. Well, what I shall do, I think, is endow a memorial prize. It will be called the Jackie Layne Memorial prize for Ethnic Minority Studies. I will resign and write that Jackie was a friend, a black woman and mother of two who killed herself in Coventry last year.

And then, quieter still: no, I am not Jackie; that would give a wrong impression. It would seem as if there was a Cause. There never was a cause. Only people. There should never have been a battlefield. I shall go forth in peace and be of good faith.

Sunday 14th June

The world is an internally consistent system, which rights itself. If you honour that system, it will honour you. "No! I will not be a receptacle for your children as yet unborn and I will not devote myself to bringing them up alone, with not even an adult to speak to. I am not that sort of container

I am a person who contains.

I will not tolerate the rape of Gaia –"

Let it be so.

Did anyone foresee the implications of an age of moral ambiguity? Some did. But how many knew what justice was? They did not know the difference between justice and sameness. You see, justice is not in getting the same as everyone else; it lies in getting what you deserve. You cannot attack people and take half of what they have; you cannot attack innocent people; you cannot take anything from them What they have is theirs.

God's justice is perfect. Man's is not. God's justice is merciful. Justice is not about revenge or even feeling better.

Allah.

God's justice teaches and protects.

And women need justice, too.

Out of the East came famine
Out of the West came strife
Out of the North came a warrior wind
And it struck me like a knife.
So the stars twinkled at His birth, and shone in His
death, and glowed in His peace forever.

Suits you, Madam.
We can offer you a choice of suits, Miss Jones.
The one's called Wife and the other Mistress.
The first one is black.
The second is glittery purple.
You will find that neither fits you.
And you mustn't mind if neither of them suits you.
In fact, people might ignore you in both
And you will be lonely and frustrated
Always waiting and isolated, but
It is all they make for women. Please, don't weep.
You can have they grey old sack they call the
Scrapheap.

And here is Bridget Kendall from Peking, with Bill Clinton.
She smiled from half way around the world.

I resign. *Diolch yn fawr a ffarwel*. Thank you and goodbye.

I made them cry for the Welsh.

I made them cry, for the Welsh the sky is crying here now, too.

Uncle Glyn, Glyn Thomas, was a graduate of Aberystwyth University. He was the youngest ever member of the Royal Geographical Society. He crossed the Sahara in a Jeep and was the headmaster of his own school. He married the French teacher, Auntie Beryl.

I do not need lessons in education from my English peers. My superiors, yes.

Melanie Klein predicted that in sixty years, neurosis would be eradicated. Bye bye neurosis.

July

J. is in Scotland and my grandmother has died.

She was almost ninety-three. I would like her to have lived into the new millennium, received a telegram from the Queen. He shows no interest here, either.

I go down to Cymmer, to be stunned by this beautiful village of ours in a narrow gorge at the head of the valley. Hairpin bends, steep, steep roads that lead me to wonder how anyone can have moved about these byways in the winter. This would include my father as a boy in callipers.

But in hearing Callum's voice in my imagination, in September, and in grasping for the words to describe it, I regained that clarity of thinking which had been obscured in sleepiness and lack of clarity, I regained the short-term memory and my control over a pen, the lack of which had been the most recent legacy of the occasion when I had dived into shallow water and hit the bottom of the pool with a smack.

Jerry is gone. I would rather have a songbird in my nest than a cuckoo.

> Hangman, stay your hand
> Oh stay it for a while
> For I think I see my true love a-coming
> Over yonder stile

Jan sings, at camp.

September 24th

Good evening, Mr Rushdie.

We see God's mercy as well as His justice.

Peace be among you. Peace be with you all.

Is it Michaelmas yet? St Michael and his dragons fought.

All is not lost. Joe is playing the piano again. Aslan is coming. I will cope. Aslan is coming.

We will go back to Cambridge. I will teach. But everything is precarious. The house is crowded. We've even brought the cats (minus one, mauled to death by a bulldog three days before we left). Joe's friend, Joe B., here for his father's sabbatical, is in a terrible bicycling accident, unconscious in the neurocritical unit of the hospital: Joe is unnerved.

God is showing me something here. I visit the church of Our Lady and the English Martyrs in Cambridge. Am encouraged to examine my thoughts; can thoughts really be sinful? It is thought to be so – desires. All these desires. Light a candle for Joe B. I look up and see a statue of St Joseph exactly in my line of sight. Joe recovers and returns to New Zealand.

Mr Blair calls it Black Christmas. Into January, a clamour clangs:

'We'll be in touch, Mrs Appleby,' 'Just send a C. V.,' 'You have failed to fulfil..,' 'The court requires...' Simon says, 'Do it, you're worth it.' Francis says, 'Oh dear, oh dear.' Alex says, 'I would like to have had a wife like you.' J. says, 'Live like an African woman.' 'But they are allowed to have husbands,' I answer. Jan says, 'We'll love one another and sing.' Jan Snowden is a singer. Marc says, 'You are a teacher,' and Ilke, a Turkish businessman student, 'You will always be my teacher,' and my babies do not think it is fun any more. Not one of the gallery of suitors is here now and none of them thinks of providing, as I would have, and have, for them. *O Jesu mawr* (O great Jesus). Only the Welsh is sufficient to convey my pain. Oh Lord, thou pluckest me.

Is it nothing to you, all ye that pass here? Kosovo... Basra...Colombia.

Knit blankets?

Over the weekend, early in February, King Hussein of Jordan is dying. I start to think what could happen after this. Well, either a war with Israel which Jordan can no longer prevent or the Arab nations fighting against themselves. God strengthens Hussein's heir Abdullah and all is well. He must travel and establish himself.

'One of these days we'll reach that river Jordan...'

> I want to cross over
> I want to cross over
> I want to cross over into
> Camp ground

One nice man. Replace him with what? Oh, another nice man!

I understand.

Makes two nice men.

Scriptus est.

It is written.

Poverty – the mind appals (William Blake). Small bits of work, small bits of cash. A bridge made of sufficiency.

Well, there are scenarios becoming clearer. Simon is Posthumus. Jerry is Iachimo, the mistrustful, beguiling friend. Joe and Henry and Jonathan have been Belarius and Arviragus and Guiderius throughout. I am Fidele, my name is Faith. I am Imogen, named Fidele est. 'When a piece of tender air...' Posthumus Leonatus. Leo is Posthumus. Cymbeline.

Kosovo – NATO – Belgrade – Serbia.

Well, Beefy the Forest School Camps chief was Duncan, the good leader, and his grandsons Jake and Jan were Donalbain and Malcolm and Jerry was the hapless friend Banquo and his son André was Fleance. Who were Macbeth and Lady Macbeth? Perhaps Alan and Rosanna – or Dennis, who usurped my promotion with so much woolly structuralism, and his Julie. Jonathan the absent, but finally worthwhile, Macduff.

We look forward to moving on.

Posthumus Leonatus est. Posthumus is born Leo. He lives at 42.42 is the answer. Leo is Aslan. But Leo is 22 (I am 42), and spiritual leader, leader of peace though he may be, I can't see Leo as Aslan, as Leo the lion. He is a charismatic member of the camping organisation.

Jerry is Mr Rochester. He has a foreign ex-partner and a bi-lingual child who reminds him of a wasted past. The dream had said that there would be a trivial halt, one caused by Annabel, but the dance would go on. The dance is soon. Is Jerry, who plays for dancing, the Lord of the Dance?

Jan is Claudio. He was told lies. 'Don Alan', the jealous half-brother, will depart in disgrace and…the dance? This scenario, from *Much Ado About Nothing*, has got a dance, too.

But look! –

There are Albanians, Kosovans, going home to their villages! And the sun is strong and the Kosovans are waving from their wagons! It is 16th June and Kosovo is free. So my thoughts are with Vera and Vjeko, and Dennis, and Marco and Bela and Mlatco and Fahrudin…and perhaps we are coming through.

It was to be a holiday. To… Yugoslavia. In 1991. Much regretted, repented. Yes, indeed it was wrong, misguided, evil. I've written to Misha to tell him that it was to have been a holiday to Yugoslavia that Alan and I were planning. And it wasn't to be, that year, or for the following eight years and now, somehow, I will be happy if it will never be at all. 'The marriage of the Lord is come. And the bride hath made herself ready for him.' The Church will be working again. It is God's gift for the millennium that there will be a whole Mother Church.

… Thanks be to God.

'Jake seems quite keen.'

'Hang on, hang on, hang on. You can't marry your brother. Jake is your brother.'

'But I love him, and he's gorgeous. He was lovely when he was a child. I loved him when we were children in Wales.'

'Can't you see that you are in the wrong plot? You can't marry Guiderius.'

'But I can't see the ending.'

'Look, what happened in Cambridge, before Christmas?'

It was a murder story. My mother was going to poison my food…

'Stick to the truth!'

My brother was the hatchet man (Pisario). Jake and Jan were Guiderius and Arviragus, the two brothers taken by their father, Tom. I said to Tom, 'Jake looks so much like my brother.' I could sense his kinship. Iachimo was Jerry (who is, in fact, J.) who tried to destroy my innocence. Posthumus must be Julian, who understands my status. My father, Cymbeline, unrecognised son not of coalminers but coalowners. My poor mother is cast as the wicked Queen. I am Imogen, whose name is Faith.

'Come, oh Lord Jesus, come.' *Jane Eyre.*

'Look, don't be an idiot. Jake is Posthumus. He put Beefy's ashes on the fire. It isn't that simple. He has more than one face. He is also Mr Rochester. He has a child. Most certainly he has a past. His parents gave him to you. You will continue a dynasty. He is of your age group. There will be room for the children, the existing ones and for more. Jonathan, Joe and Henry are Belarius, Arviragus and Guiderius. Jake is not your brother, he is your husband.'

It fits. It fits. It is a fitting conclusion; the Lamb and the Lion are as one.

So, people like Mr Aaronovitch, the journalist (who was at Beefy's memorial), Dan Cutler (my ruthless ex-boyfriend, who almost toppled Jonathan), Melissa Benn (who was

Dan's exgirlfriend), my hard but fair friends, we have delivered an age. It is an age of people, not of types, having the virtues of honesty, integrity and realism. It is an age which knows that a smile cannot feed a million mouths and knows the difference between a negotiated settlement and a fudge. It will be an age of real justice and real mercy; of true conciliation, re-building, reunion.

East Timor – UN.

In Cambridge, before Christmas, there was a huge argument over Joe and Henry. Jonathan put insistent pressure on me to see them more, even though they were only just settling into their new home. I ask them to play on their computer more quietly and they don't comply. I ask more loudly. Nothing. I demand, I shout once and my mother appears: 'Oh, the neighbours, the children, oh me, you'll have to go.' She passes out on the bed.

My brother is summoned and evicts us. I go to the Midlands, where the house is not yet sold and Joe and Henry go to Jonathan's, opting to stay there rather than return, with more embarrassment more than their age can tolerate, to their previous school.

I spend 1999 alone, with very little money. The money I had for the children has been discontinued and I cannot pay the bills.

I can now let you know the real ending. In the year 2000 he will return from the east with the golden sun; like the sun, indeed actually as the sun. This is a promise of justice, as believed in the Middle East, where graves face eastwards in anticipation of his return. A king. He will come from the East. Does this sound too much like Atahualpa?

Justan is a king. Well, a kind of prince, really.

A Kitchener, he is royalty. A friend from Forest School Camps. He is coming home, home from Burma now and the light around me, through me and out into the garden is bouncing against the wall, is a brilliant, bright, scented beam, white, yes, like a diamond, a brilliant, perfumed, white. 'She loved us,' say the children. A reference to the fact that I looked after Justan when he was a child.

But Justan has not returned by the fourth of September. Today it would have been my grandmother's ninety-fourth birthday. Instead, Jake and I are looking at each other across the campfire. Jo and I have sorted the world out again this evening as we always do and I hope that everyone is learning to find a place of their own. Jake's son is magnificent – real and wonderful. I have never seen so many stars amassed in the sky. On Thursday it will be 9.9.99 and will we see the end of world evil? – the inverted 666 ('let him who understands...') which was 'the mark of the devil'. The perversion of emergency aid. A ceasefire is reported in Israel. Orthodox Jews tell us that there will not be a lasting peace in Israel until the coming of the Messiah.

Thoughts still centre on Justan. 'She loved us beyond drugs and rubbish and things.' Justan is Charles of *The French Lieutenant's Woman*; where he was previously sick and anxious, he is now travelled and calm. Charles finds Sarah civilised and happy in London. In Chelsea. Justan lives in Fulham, next to Chelsea, on the river, near to Cheyne Walk, where Jasper lived, who had a living belief in God, was my first partner, was alpha and here now is omega. Justan brings frankincense. He is the black king, an aristocratic Indian, who acknowledges God with incense. Justan is surely Posthumus and returns. Surely he will return? He brings peace and prosperity to Lud's Town, returning the lost children and establishing right order, the line of ascendancy and the rule of law. The smoke is rising over London. All is well. Amen to this.

I can see it all. But then, I've read the play. Jasper is Charles?

Peter is returning from the east. He has been a correspondent in India for about five years.

Peter is good news. Mr Rochester. Posthumus.

Hugh is Hugh Grant! Hugh Smith, another friend from camp. He is a handsome student, just like the character in the film *Notting Hill*. I am Julia Roberts! How does the film end? I haven't seen it!

Jeremy is Posthumus. How? We were innocent together. Once. And Jeremy has not yet discovered innocence beyond experience.

Jake is Posthumus.

He receives my postcard about Damien, who reprimanded me for loving him. I signed it 'hate' in irony (not 'love'). Damien is another camper. Jake is Aslan! He shifts in and out of the action, turning up as the spirit moves and bringing peace and security. I was chosen. To reinforce this, it rains and hails at the same time in a merry confusion and the sun is shining, too. It is Jake and it fits.

Now I see Damien's role. I knew him over the difficult turn of the millennium, so-called.

I had rented a flat in London to be near the children. Just for two or three months. That was all I could afford. Damien was the feeling behind the 'millennium' when the sun showed its dual nature by rising continuously in the news for 24 hours while staying ceremoniously in the same place. I told Dan, we have a poetic as well as a scientific model of the universe. Damien and I planned a venture together and it gave me hope. But Damien was a driven man. I told him I loved him and he roasted me.

'Haven't you heard of romance?' I asked him. I might as well have said, 'I spurn your counterfeit idea of love.' If you know *Jane Eyre*, you will see that there it is. Damien is St John Rivers to Jake's Mr Rochester. Attractive and finally cold. Not as attractive as Mr Roch – I mean Jake, as it happens. But that fits the popular view of the character. Also in London is Leo. Leo is Claudio. It was mutual love at first sight. Or wild passion and joy. Leo is at 42 and this lovely, happy, talented man is the answer. Jeremy will play Don John. The conclusion is that, well, I think we are asked to take Leo seriously. He is an angel. A real one. His brother, an angel, too, Fergus, lulls me to sleep. He knows and accepts, is kind and is mild.

I send them a Christmas card from the Angel, Islington.

The children visit. I have a funny little job conducting a sex survey. The respondents are mortally embarrassed to have been selected and will not talk and it will not pay the bills.

The landlady smells blood where there is none and goes for the kill. I jump over her iron railings and escape once more to Cambridge. I cannot get a job in teaching. The supply teachers' contract has a clause about student complaints and I have to declare them. Even though they weren't true, were palpable nonsense, I cannot teach. This is redeemed by the fact that later I am granted an ill health pension which states that I must not teach in order to qualify. On these conditions, I am all too happy to give up what was always a dreadful if interesting burden. I can do my funny little job in Cambridge, where people will talk to researchers.

But I will not go further until I have given you the ending.

2000

It is May. How can my life make sense without Joe and Henry's company?

It is May and there are three medics at the door and two ambulancemen. I have a few minutes to get some things and telephone a solicitor before I am bundled into the back of an ambulance and am heading for the psychiatric hospital.

It is quite nice. Beautiful, large grounds. Excellent weather. Restful. Apart from the bullying and the deprivation. Asking for a mug to drink out of, I am given a dirty old beer glass. The night staff talk all night. One is checked every hour (I had hoped it would settle my sleep). I have no summer clothes. Sophie kindly brings some when I tell her that I am not in touch with my family any more. I plead to the hospital for five pounds – finally the hospital arranges for my sister to cash a cheque. For three days I am under constant surveillance. If I move, a shadowy nurse armed with bunches of keys moves with me. I'm not aware why. Is it 'suicide watch' or part of the assessment? Jonathan will not allow the children to talk to me. I had turned against my mother in a mock show of anger and it has all been taken much too far. Yes, there are feelings. But I have feelings, too. The psychiatrist affirms that I am a patient, not a prisoner, and am there for my protection. I have been brought here under the Mental Health Act on the basis of the 'evidence' of my family and that evidence is not true.

Which is not to say that I am not ill. I am not qualified to have opinion on that.

A nurse tells me casually and informally that the diagnosis is probable schizophrenia.

But perhaps I will benefit. I decide to go along with things. After all, it is I who have been asking for support for all these years. I think of the many times when the offer of help with a little shopping would have been so welcome. It was this dangerous to go home to my family. It is, actually, very, very frightening and still so good to meet so many funny, sociable people. We watch the football matches together. There is a dance. Five weeks pass. I am given drugs and have no choice but to take them – or be injected, which frightens me more. I get through this and am allowed out again, to the shops and, yes, to my mother's. We have patched together a reconciliation. I may go home soon. I will need to find a home – and work. But God pumps His spirit through me and I cannot feel too bad.

The two Williams sisters will fight. We see the power of women's strength and rivalry.

And here is one of the nurses. It is Steve; he is holding a letter for me. It is an airmail letter…one from India. Steve is holding a letter to me from Peter.

March 2004

I spent three years establishing myself in Cambridge. I
got a flat, I wrote a lot of poems I was fairly happy with. I
think the best way of filling in this space is to refer you to
the poems. You can trace the influences – I identified with
Sylvia Plath for several obvious reasons, I have a hill at the
end of my garden and I watch the elements and seasons,
sun over wood, light across field, huge moon tonight.
Worldwise, we did not cope with Muslims and they did
not cope with us. The terrorists, anyway. You may note that
September 11th is our wedding anniversary. We went to war.
Children, including Joe and Henry, demonstrated. Henry
was to be found one day not in his school but protesting in
Parliament Square. I demonstrated, too, but not for the sake
of Saddam Hussein. I was rather glad he got caught. I went
for humanitarian reasons and to show that adults can do it
responsibly and because war does not produce peace, will it
though we will.

Oh, you'll be wondering about the letter from Peter.
In hasty writing he told me that yes, he was in love with
Arundati Roy as I'd guessed, though he hadn't seen her with
her new hairstyle. And that he'd been a brat not to reply to
my letters, they were interesting. It cheered me up to be in
touch. I didn't see The News that day. And things improved
and I worked at things I hadn't had time for, church, music,
poetry. Joe and Henry thrived with Jonathan in London.
I missed them and saw them when I could. I cared for my
mother. We developed a *modus vivendi*. She is very kind to
me and I am grateful. I went back and forth for therapy.
I didn't change my views. So perhaps I'll never get better!
Sometimes I felt unbearably lonely.

Do you know how lonely it felt in that tomb, three days,
cold, alone?

Was there ever a world without depression? So what is this appalling and wonderful clarity? Let me tell you about James, the curate of my church. He shares my experience of English Literature, in a big way. Big enough to have taught it at Cambridge University.

My love of God and Christ, of course. My involvement with the emotions. He is a bereavement counsellor. I told you something about Melanie Klein. Not enough, probably. You have to clock the ideas about paranoia and depression. Paranoia is a failure to mourn. Depression unstuck is the process of mourning. We pass from paranoia to depression by developing feelings for our mother as a 'whole person', who 'contains' us and helps us adapt to reality. Think feminist. I am not 'a pert blonde'. I am a woman. Last night I felt that my mother let go of me – no more worry, no more control – or that I separated from her, or both – Hey! New life in Cambridge flat scenario! Today, James rang. This evening, as I prepared to cook my courgettes in garlic, my steak in black pepper, my corn on the cob, it cleared – something in relation to James, nothing specific – the mourning cleared. The dripping, sodden, warm wetness of my eyes cleared and I got a clear as a bell, pure as a mountain stream, ticking over like an engine mind back and Tony Blair is shaking Colonel Gaddafi's hand in a roadside picnic in a tent with camels on a scrubby patch of land in Libya that looks like somewhere off the M4 near Reading.

It is the August Bank Holiday. In London, I see a shrine at Harrods to Di and Dodi. It is seven years since their death. The princess and her handsome Muslim prince. I write to mine, wondering if the spirit is there.

I always loved you. I never stopped. I always will. I have sent you petals and a poem and my love. Will you send me yours? We probably all know the ending about the 'ten thousand violins' and the 'unplumbed, salt, estranging sea'.

And perhaps we have seen the only Shakespeare play to end with a dance.

It did not end with a dance. It ended with 333 people, mostly children, being killed in a stuffy, dehydrated, starving school in Beslan. I am sick. I am absolutely disgusted. There is no excuse for this. I will not put up with any more.

I can feel Peter again. I can also feel tolerant and balanced again. It is essential that Peter's influence is brought to bear, tolerant, reasonable, effective. The tradition of British investigative journalism. I connect with Peter. I want to explain to him that it might be masochistic to care so much about racism – it is too painful – that I had been trying to protect myself, evidently not very effectively, in a new way. At the same time, I had been working for harmony. I want to tell him that there might be in some ways real, but not insurmountable, differences between peoples or parts of people. That what we must know is that the similarities are greater than the differences. I have finally got the message. Find someone like Peter. He knows the difference between good and evil. He is good.

'Britain's sporting hero, Jonny Wilkinson, returns' says the BBC News, Sunday 5 September 2004.

'Sorry, Peter.'

'Sorry, Linda.'

Spring 2005

Jan is appearing at the Folk Festival, which is virtually in my back garden. We had lost touch. I wrote to him telling him it was too stressful for me. That's all it was. But now, I can see it all. He is The Voice. Jan is Claudio. I fell in love. It was poisoned by the jealous Don J. I had to leave the camps and London. But now I can see him. It clears – this is a tale of international understanding. He knows we are not peasants. I can give him my lyrics… It is pregnant with possibilities. I can come back to the camps in an appropriate role, singing, catering, not as a beginner.

I give you the dance!

Tomorrow is Election Day. The Pope is dead. Peter writes all about it. Charles and Camilla are married. Isn't that about taking marriage seriously?

Bush is back. The Iraq affair goes on. Joe is a student. Henry is a guitarist. And at least the man, for it will be a man, who will be elected tomorrow stands a chance of being nice. There goes Maoism. There goes China. There goes sameism. Is he nice? He is threatening my benefit.

The lady in Tesco's tells me, 'There's a special offer on Comfort today.' I think my time is coming.

'There's a special offer on Comfort today.'
I think I'll have some cheap to help me on my way
I Will Come
I will come to you
When the wheat is waxing in the field
When the sun is fixed in a sapphire sky
I will come to you
When the fruit is ripening on the heavy trees
And the pheasant's eggs have hatched in the nest
And the pink of the geranium stuns
I will come to you,
When the roses are ready
And the river swells with roach
And the dogs lie panting in the outhouse
When my time is coming
I will come to you
When the car comes for the nervous bride
When the end of time begins

Jim, in the singing group, is looking great today. We get on so well. But he can't be much older than Joe. I can't do that to my son. The young men seem to think that there's some happiness to be gained by going to bed with someone without a relationship. I can't imagine anything more miserable. It is a constant source of tension. Knock at the door. 'Would I like my doorstep delivery returned?' 'Yes, please, because I feel guilty about getting milk at the supermarket.' I led Bible Study this morning. It felt good. We studied the story of Noah's ark. God promised never to threaten mankind again. So has He delivered us from the threat of nuclear war? And I can have fun with Jim? Jan has not surfaced. He must be a sub-plot. Rosemary and I will meet in London in September for a Water-Aid singing event. The two sisters... the Nice Man. In London. Everyone is to wear white. Rosemary will have two white salwar kameez made in Moleshill Road and we will dress identically for the first time since I was about six. And afterwards I propose to meet Peter in a nice Thai restaurant in Upper Street, Islington. He was a writer for the *Independent*. I was a *Guardian* reader. He feared a third world war might break out between us and he went away. It never did. I hope it never will.

And now I can see why Jim is good. It is because, almost simply, he would care about the issues in this book. He cared about the article I wrote about losing my job. The fixed Disciplinary Hearing. The witch hunt. He simply assumed I was innocent. He cares about good and evil and war and peace and truth and lies. He held my hand when I told the group about my job. So I will finish this book so that he can have a copy and read it.

11th June

A letter has arrived from Abbas, who taught at the mosque in Nuneaton. He tells me he has experienced a miracle: after ten years of dialysis, a kidney has become available and after initial problems it is now functioning. Give thanks to the Lord. 'Thank you, kind Lord,' writes Abbas. The man who taught me the meaning of the word 'respect' has been saved. It is not a quick fix. It is a life of worship and sacrifice. We had forged those links a decade ago. They tried to destroy them. We were both broken-hearted and, yes, disillusioned. 'And when the broken-hearted people living in the world agree there will be an answer. Let it be.'

Peter and I had commiserated about divorce and children. I told him there was an answer.

We had been broken-hearted.

Today I felt a new depth of care arrive for me. It wasn't that there was no care before, but as if something at the centre of me which had been plundered and drained had been restored. For the first time in my life I felt I could love a man like a woman and not just be admired. Now I understand and the atmosphere is light and joyful and the people in church are joyful because their life source has been replenished. It is almost as if it is my smile which is being restored.

'Blessed is the woman whose strength is in thee; in whose heart are the ways of them. Who passing through the valley of tears make it a well; the rain also filleth the pools.' Psalm.

The Queen, in pink and black, arrives at Ascot (York) in a carriage, in a shiver of excitement, as the National Anthem strikes up and one reflects on her incredible reign.

And on a fluttery, warmish day in Cambridge, words of love wing their way from Rome.

Someone believes me at last: 'Linda was a writer!' It is as if Alan has confessed, I am at the centre of a wonderful romance and the innocent (including Michael Jackson) are released all over the world.

Jan is a proper man. He could substitute for Jonathan. I imagine that we might risk trying again. The temperature rises for the first time in a week or so. It has been pouring with rain. In *Othello*, Emilia muses: 'Lodovico was a proper man. I would walk barefoot to Palestine...' Or is she too forward and worldly? It actually started with my bare feet! Jan and I were singing in a group sitting on the grass. The temperature was in the 90s. I took my shoes off...

Then the royal connection suggests Justan. Is it he who I will meet in September? The return of the Muslims, the Queen's arrival at Ascot...but he's not a Muslim, as far as I know. His smile was like the most precious gift of jewels. It is about respect for the small peoples of the earth, whatever group they might belong to, whatever they believe. The meek will, after all, inherit the earth.

Politics is dead. The feeling I have travelled hundreds of miles for is here in my sitting room. Remember that phrase, the withering away of the state? All there is, is the wild thudding of the wind across the hills, uninterrupted by the structures of mankind. Where the wind blows, there am I. Chop wood, eat well, sit round the fire in the evening, live to the full. Contrast this with the rubbish about meaninglessness. Sing and play. Be a man in relation to your God. Myself, a burning candle and the hills. Joe and Henry. Who can be as God to me? Or with God? My therapist? Peter? Daniel? Attachments wither. Zen sets in.

I couldn't do the 'return to nature' stuff so easily in London. Or in Cambridge. I had a more suburban personality there. Now who is it who brings in the summer and my church's 50th anniversary but Jonathan, whose name really is Jonathan? He is my friend in the Welsh class. A practicing Anglican, who values learning. He even looks like Peter. The temperature soars. We welcome the new, black Archbishop of York. And forgiveness, which is what the whole Christian revolution was supposed to be about and love, similarly, flood the earth. People will be able to apologise. The sons and daughters of Abraham shine in the night sky And there is an army of saints ready to run the show. 'There is an answer,' I told Peter. 'They understand divorce. The children will be OK.'

Jim has gone to Edinburgh for the G8 protest. So have Rosemary and Philip. Antecedent to the ending of this story are London's two days of agony and ecstasy. People from our North London haunts are incinerated in four bombings. Do you see now why I don't support terrorism? Why I gave my love to J., who worked in the Metropolitan Police in North London? Let's try and sort out our attitudes. Londoners wearing Make Poverty History' wristbands are lying dead under city streets. Let's try and make sense. Take politics seriously. Thank goodness Joe and Henry slept through the bombings.

Wander around the Botanic Gardens looking for the iris beds. Am taken back to my old school friend Lesly, who used to come here at lunchtimes from school and walk around the rockery. I go to my school reunion lunch. Sue tells me that Lesly would like to be in touch. She is ill. It has been thirty years. I contact Lesly and a perfect, clear rainbow forms across the field, with a fainter rainbow accompanying on the outside. Bombs. Six houses searched in Leeds and a car found at Luton station. Please, let them not be British Muslims. But they are. Look, I say to my Muslim friends, it's OK to say that Jesus was divine. The Trinity is just an expression of different forms of God, which is Love. There is only one God, in three manifestations. There is, in fact, a stranger point of agreement: no-one wants to worship a real person! But Christ is the commonality which will solve everything. Just unravel a few tiles and you will see. Do you see why it was so necessary to take people seriously and not inflame things? The police and the army are doing amazing work. They are protecting us. They will win. Jonathan arrives home on his bike from the West End. He is proud of the security forces too. The security level today is 'critical', the highest level and never used before. Jonathan and I agree on the protection of the children. They are safe.

Victor has died. He took us to The Hebrides thirty years ago this month. It was where I met Dave and Daniel. Victor was a friend of my father's and my friend's father-in-law. We will go, Dad, Joe, Henry and myself, to the Quaker memorial service in London in September. In the spirit of unity which has followed the bombings of 7th July, George has forgiven me my partly-Indian-inspired ideas on the purpose of God. 'Oh I see, the purpose is to help others in the same situation.' Yes, that sort of purpose. And he has forgiven my thinking he was with another woman in church. 'George, I just can't believe you are mine.'

Well, he's not, it seems. What you need to understand is the sexual transference; the sexualizing of a relationship, quite unconsciously. But has the relationship completely died in all this?

And I try to forgive those who treat me as if I have no status because I have no man.

So, I will be going to Victor's service and singing for Water Aid. Then Jan will come to the stores weekend at Haddenham, near here, and we will sing and play. We will lay down the coffin of political exploitation and turn to the fire of tolerance and compassion.

'Four suicide bombers have been arrested and the IRA announces the end of terrorist activity. The Parliamentary road.

I have met A Nice Man. Well, he seems nice, anyway.

We just looked at each other and said 'Hello!'

All the things in my world are telling me I have found it: I have found my pens and keys. I lost my purse in the supermarket, cheque cards, cash, photographs of Joe and Henry. Next day, it had been handed in, quite intact. I lost the car in the car park and found it by intuition on Level C when my intellect told me it was on Level D. I lost my sandwiches and found them in my mother's fridge. And in the evening, the moon hangs effaced and low, like a copper coin assuming the guise of a planet, in a powder-blue sky, the trees are silhouettes in silence and my upright, new candle is reflected in the window like a Christmas tree light, like Pepper's Ghost. It is a sublime evening in a Japanese garden. On the CD player, John Lennon is singing 'There will be an answer...' 'There will be light at evening time,' said my mother. Let it be so.

Israelis are evacuating Israelis from Gaza.

Jesus relaxed and sadly said,
'The devil made me hate the world
And now I've got to love it more instead.'
'It's hard,' he said, 'even for Gods
When all you meet is bitterness,
Greed and envy, hate, impatience,
People who want their own remittance.'
Jesus sighed and grimly said,
'I'll have to drill up yet more love
And face the final battle over him,'

And the sun shone more in the sky above.